Few men have led a life like that of Les Nichols. In *Confessions of a Name Dropper*, Nichols provides an insider's account on some of the most significant men and moments of American history.

A graduate of Dartmouth College, Nichols served our nation at its greatest time of need, first as a Platoon Leader in the 2nd Armored Division and later as a Tank Company Commander with the 3rd Armored Division under the command of General George Patton. Highlights of his World War II experiences include capturing German Field Marshal Wilheim List and liberating 6000 Prisoners of War at Memmigen Prison Camp in Southern Bavaria. The Bronze Star, the French Croix and campaign ribbons for the Battle of the Bulge are just a few of the honors bestowed upon this veteran whose professional career was as distinguished as his military career.

Nichols gained notoriety as the author of *Impact*, the official battle story of Patton's spearhead Armored Division. Other works include *You are the West Point Story*, prepared for the U.S. Military Academy; *How To Tell It*, a media guide for New York area colleges and universities; and *Terrify and Destroy*, an account of the 10th Armored "Tiger" Division. His knowledge of military history helped establish Les Nichols as a leading consultant and adviser on a variety of projects. He has served as a Technical Adviser for Warner Brothers Studios as well as Broadway's war play, *Fragile Fox*.

Les Nichols went on to launch his own public relations firm, which held accounts with organizations such as the Kentucky Heart Association, Arthritis Foundation, the American Red Cross, The Kentucky Hotel-Motel Association, and the Louisville Motel & Hotel Association. He also worked with a score of celebrities like Roy Rogers, Bobby Riggs, and Jackie Robinson...just to name a few.

Through *Confessions*, Nichols shares the lasting impressions of the people and places which have so richly penetrated his life experiences.

Confessions

of a Name Dropper

by

Les Nichols

TURNER PUBLISHING COMPANY

Turner Publishing Company

Copyright © 1999
Lester M. Nichols
Publishing Rights: Turner Publishing Company

Liabrary of Congress Catalog
Card No: 99-066915
ISBN: 978-1-68162-595-9

Table of Contents

Dedicated To

Those valiant combat heroes of World War II
who gave up their tomorrows so that
we might have our todays.

and

Edie, Nancy, and Karen
the three most important
people in my life

Offices Held

Former Newsletter Editor of the Dartmouth Class (1940)

Press Officer of Tenth Armored Division (1942-1945)

Technical Advisor for Warner Brothers Studio (1943)

Combat Briefing Officer for General George S. Patton's staff (1944-1945)

Assistant to the President, City College of New York (1947-1954)

Press Manager, National Horse Show at Madison Square Garden (1948-1953)

Special Events Director, Greater New York Fund (1950-1954)

President, Metropolitan College Public Relations Council (1951)

Technical Advisor, Broadway Play Fragile Fox (1954)

Chairman, American College Public Relations Association (1954)

Former State Campaign Chairman with KY Heart Association (1955-1980)

Former Secretary Dartmouth Club of Louisville (1957-1959)

State Campaign Director, Arthritis Foundation (1960-1978)

National President, Tenth Armored Division Association (1961-1963)

Executive Director, Printing Industries of Kentucky (1972-1974)

Adjutant, Military Order of World War II (1985-1986)

Director, Kentucky Society of Association Executives (1986-1989)

Chairman, Council of Armored Divisions Associations (1997-2000)

Acknowledgments

The author is appreciative of the services of his
secretary of thirty years, Mrs. Elah Duemler,
and his neighbor, Mrs. Joan Russ, for their assistance
on "Confessions of a Name Dropper"

Confessions of a Name Dropper

Confessions of a Name Dropper

by Lester M. Nichols

A decade ago, I began writing *Confessions of a Name Dropper* but because of my heavy work schedule, only five chapters had been completed. After retiring in 1993, I began work on the book again. I had a call from Byron Crawford, columnist for the *Courier-Journal* who asked to do an interview for his column. I found him to be a very pleasant and interesting person.

His column was about some of the stories in *Confessions*. He asked how far I had progressed on the book, and I replied, "There is a great deal more to do." Byron quietly lectured me. "Why don't you prioritize and complete the book?" His gentle lecture spurred me to make the book as project number one. Needless to say, I am so glad to have received this encouragement.

The major thrust of *Confessions* was to share a large number of exclusive stories about 50 national and international celebrities in entertainment, military, political, sports and business giants. All accounts are humorous. Some are brief, others are lengthy. I felt that it would be fun to share these exclusive accounts with the readers.

I was reluctant to include chapters on growing up in Colorado and the first two decades of my life but the publisher convinced me that in doing so, it would help to explain my careers in five different professional areas.

My military career was the beginning of many different careers that included besides the military: fund-raising, sports, promotion, media relations, business, education, political and entertainment that proved most interesting and rewarding and permitted me to become involved with so many successful and prominent people in all of the above career areas. I do hope readers will enjoy these humorous anecdotes about very serious personalities.

The First Decade

Growing up in the mountains of Colorado, I can distinctly remember things that happened in my life. Yet, today, sometimes I start to do something and forget what it was I wanted to do!

Some of the earliest memories were going on hiking trips with my father and two brothers. My father began as a mining engineer (and later switched over to civil engineering) and was a very studious man. He was also a naturalist and on our hiking trips, he would describe in detail, all the flowers, shrubs, trees and bushes. At night he would tell us all about the stars and planets as we lay on our backs on a mountain top, looking up to the heavens at night. He would cut branches from birch trees and made whistles that really worked. Once, we went on a mountain hike and were walking after dark when suddenly, he told us to stop in our tracks. "Don't move a foot," he commanded. We put down our bed rolls and went to sleep right away because we ached all over from climbing. The next morning our father shook us awake and said, I thought something was wrong." What appeared just several yards away was a steep precipice which could easily have claimed our lives if it were not for his perception of danger.

I can further remember walking home from our one room schoolhouse in the afternoon. As I neared the ranch, I could smell sour dough bread that my mother baked behind the fireplace. To this day, I never smelled anything so great as her bread. She would cover the warm bread with peanut butter that even now I relish.

When I was very young, my father put me on a horse (no saddle). He whacked the animal on the butt and we would go trotting down the mountain trail. I'm not at all sure if I enjoyed hanging on to the horses mane for dear life.

I must have been bad at times because when my dad came home, mother would tell him of my misdeeds. As a result, I was taken to the bathroom where my father took off his belt and whacked me several times on the rear. I screamed more from the threat of further strapping than in actual pain, so my dad would stop. Strangely, I was never afraid of him because I knew I deserved the punishment.

Winters were harsh. The only heat in the ranch was from the kitchen stove and the fireplaces. Yet, I do not remember being so cold as I was later in life on a blustery cold damp day while in New York City at the Battery. There was no electricity, an outhouse and the barn with cows and horses were connected. Speaking of the outhouse, the slick Sears Roebuck catalog pages did little to imitate toilet paper and in the winter, it took courage to manage nature's calls.

In the wintertime when the ranch was covered with snow, I'm sure that it could not be seen from the air. Actually, the heavy snow served as a blanket similar, perhaps, to an igloo. My dad would grind up dried corn and with sugar, it made a decent breakfast. I did not know what candy, hamburgers or cokes were. We ate fresh meat and fresh vegetables from the garden. So, for my first formative years, our diet was perfect, which served us well in later life.

Unfortunately, my mother was often ill and hospitalized from severe depression, and, as a result, being the youngest of three brothers, was packed off to North Dakota to spend the summer with my Aunt Florence, a wonderful lady. She and her husband treated me as their own child. The down side though was the very cold climate at Fargo! My father pinned a tag on my coat with my name and instructions to put me off at the station at Fargo where I would be picked up by my father's sister and her husband.

I still remember being with very tall people and all strangers. Yet there was a plus in this adventure. Sweet old ladies would ask me to sit with them and would give me homemade cookies. When we arrived at Fargo, the conductor would take me by the hand to the station platform and, I think, made my aunt sign for me before he released me to yet another adventure. I was used to being alone. My brothers were older and did not want to play with the "kid," and the children I knew from school lived miles away. I enjoyed reading, having learned very early in life, and would lie on a rug by the fireplace, which shed enough light for me to see the words. Even when I was in grade school, I would visit the library and take out four or five books a week.

The Second Decade

When I was about 10 years old we moved from Colorado to St. Paul, Minnesota and then to Scranton, Pennsylvania. My father was in a constant search for better job opportunities. It seemed that I was never in the same school for more than a year, just as I made friends, we moved. I can remember when I was ready to take on the boys in my class when they laughed at my Colorado twang. When we moved to Scranton, I remember many experiences but the best of them was when I joined a Boy Scout troop. I was used to hiking, so when the troop went on a long hike, I was usually out in front. I worked hard to earn scout badges and it was a proud day for me when they made me an Eagle Scout.

Our overnight camping trips in the Pocano Mountains were fun and I learned to cook in a big iron skillet. One of my favorites was what I called "Colorado Stew." I would first cook a slab of bacon, then cook hamburger. After that, I would layer baked beans, hamburger and the bacon on top. When you are hungry and in the mountain air, I can assure you that nothing would be left of our Colorado treat!

I enjoyed our time in Scranton, but then we moved to East Rutherford, New Jersey where my father landed a job as chief engineer for a fledgling roofing company known as the Flintcote Company (later to become the nation's largest roofing company).

In grade school I began playing baseball and basketball. My older brother, Nick, was captain of the high school basketball team and my other brother, Art, was a good athlete. I played sports with them and, of course, they banged me around all the time. But this was good for me when I played against boys my own age, and I later captained my Westchester County, New York, junior high school team to the championship.

This leads again, to another move to White Plains. By this time, my older brother Nick had a very bad falling out with my father, who was away most of the time on his professional career, and my mother was in a hospital in New Jersey. Now there were three of us alone and my brother Art and I shared a room in a rooming house in White Plains. We moved to New Rochelle, New York in 1932 and though I wanted more than anything to play high school basketball and football, I was hindered by having to work every night at Schrafts' upscale restaurant in order to pay for my room and meals. Despite this problem, I had a great chance to make the high school team until the authorities determined I was ineligible because of grades thanks to one particular teacher who would go on to make a great impact on my life.

Two Teachers

Most students in their school years had teachers they liked or disliked, and I was no exception to the rule. I particularly remember a teacher (I think it was in the sixth grade) who, no matter the quality of my answers to her questions would respond with great praise. She made me feel excited to do better, and I did try do better and earn her praise. She made me feel good about being a student even if I was perhaps, a notch above mediocrity.

On the other hand, the teacher I had in math in high school was without question, a person you could easily hate. Her name was Miss Treadwell. Even now six decades later, her mark on me is never forgotten. Miss Treadwell was a tall spinster lady wearing thick glasses and was formidable and tough. She could put an Army drill sergeant to shame; she was that tough. She was in her late 50s and had a reputation that advised students to avoid her class.

1936 New Rochelle, N.Y. High School Team

At that time in my life, my primary interest was in sports. I studied just enough to barely make "C" grades. It was just my luck to get Miss Treadwell as my teacher. In class she would insult me at every turn. "You are the dumbest and laziest boy I have ever taught," she would say, and added, "you will never amount to anything."

It was very easy to put her on top of my hate list. As the term progressed, she made me stay after school and miss football practice. At that time, I had a good shot in making first string halfback. Then she increased my level of hatred for her when she checked on my credits and had me kicked off the team as a result of being short of enough hours in one of my classes. That did it! I was so mad at her that I decided to show her what I could do.

For the first time, I really paid attention in all my classes (and this was my senior year). After class, Miss Treadwell kept several students in her class and tutored them. On occasion, I would surprise her with correct answers, she would not compliment me and insisted I could do better. My main motivation was to prove her wrong in assessing my capabilities. I looked forward to the day when my efforts would prevent her from throwing critical darts my way. Never, at that time, did I appreciate or like her.

After some time, she would drop a kind remark, like giving a treat to a dog. She began talking about college and a slight chance that I could get a scholarship. At that time, I had no money, no influential friends and very little hope of higher education. But then the big day came in my senior year at exam time. As a result of my hatred for Miss Treadwell I received all straight "A's" and even had a chance for a scholarship.

Miss Treadwell did have influential friends and persuaded two of them to take a look at the dumb, worthless student she originally said I was. One influential person was a former all American quarterback at Dartmouth who became a senior officer of the New York Chase Manhattan Bank; the other person was the head of an education foundation in New York. Both persons questioned my grades (three years of C's and one year of A's). Over all, this record was questionable, but Miss Treadwell reasoned with them that I proved in my senior year that I was college material.

Dartmouth is one of the few colleges and universities that has alumni groups throughout the country to interview prospective students. Although this approval of student applicants does not guarantee admittance, their reports to the admissions office do help. I met with the alumni group and with a pocket full of hope did all I could to impress them.

Fortunately, I was chosen as one of the three applicants from the group of 15 who applied. As for Miss Treadwell, my math teacher. At first I hated her, but it finally dawned on me that she was one of the most influential persons in my life. She knew exactly how to psych me. First by insults, second by encouragement and third by making it possible for me to get my degree. A fact that was totally unimaginable during my first two years in high school. After my graduation in the Class of 1940 I was sent an induction letter and then served in three different armored divisions in World War II.

I did not return from U.S. occupation in Southern Bavaria until November

1945. There was one more important task for me at that time. It was to visit Miss Treadwell, the spinster lady that, in spite of me, changed my life. I called the New Rochelle high school to get her telephone number and they reported a shocking development. She had retired and moved away in 1944. So many times, I have thought about her and what she did for me and yet, I was never able to tell her how very much I appreciated her for helping me to find that educational door of opportunity. Perhaps, she knows that her resentful pupil came to understand her teaching magic. Hatred was replaced by great respect and a grateful appreciation of a former teacher.

Thus, there were two teachers in my life. Each had their own way of teaching. One taught by praise, the other taught by insult, but both succeeded.

Dartmouth College

Founded by Eleazar Wheelock in 1769, Dartmouth is located in New Hampshire on a plain with the Connecticut River flowing along the edges of the college.

Dartmouth, one of the oldest colleges in America, was the beneficiary of a land grant given by King George of England of several thousand acres. This grant was challenged by New Hampshire and resulted in an emotional plea in the U.S. Supreme Court whose verdict protected the grant. Daniel Webster, Dartmouth graduate, distinguished statesman and U.S. Senator, argued, "Dartmouth is a small college but there are those who love it." This was a landmark case that protected the rights of all institutions given land grants by the king.

I arrived there as a freshman in 1936 with no idea of how I could generate enough money to pay for tuition, board and food, but as an eternal optimist, and with the help of a scholarship, I managed to get by. Barely! When I arrived, the first person I met when I was at the bank was President Ernest Martin Hopkins. This distinguished educator was regarded by our class of 1940 as the "students" president. His door was always open, even to pea green freshman!

Perhaps no Dartmouth president agonized more than Dr. Hopkins as he watched our class go to war in 1940. He wrote letters to every one in our class expressing his concern for our safety and well being. It was almost for him as a father, seeing his boys go off to an uncertain future. In 1990, I was asked to write a "War Diary" of the class.

I have never been more proud (in researching) of my classmates who distinguished themselves in the Army, Navy, Air Force and Coast Guard. Our losses were extremely heavy. We have never forgotten the ultimate price these brave men paid in battle in Western Europe and the Pacific.

Now, back to 1936 at Dartmouth. I was forced to find jobs in order to stay in college. During my freshman year, I worked in Ma Smalley's eating club, sold programs at football games, delivered the *New York Herald Tribune* to professors homes at 6:00 a.m. with winter temperatures often at zero or below. In fact, I was involved in so many projects that I never thought of "who am I," or what my future might hold.

During our sophomore year, I inherited better jobs as a result of seniors who graduated. Still, I barely managed to stay in school because of fund problems.

During my junior and senior years, the situation improved to the extent that I was hiring freshmen and sophomores for jobs I used to do. My fledgling laundry business soared with more than 25 students on my payroll. I helped register students as they arrived for the school year, monitored exams, refereed high school baseball games, sold sandwiches in the dorms at night and worked about six hours a day besides going to classes. You ask, "when did I have time to study." The answer is that my study hours were from 11:00 p.m. until 1:30 a.m.

This may sound difficult. It wasn't because in our dorm, students were sometimes playing hockey in the corridors or visiting the rooms for bull sessions. It was difficult to study because of the noise during the early evening. By 11:00 p.m. the dorm was silent and I was able to complete my class assignments. The dean of the college shook hands with me at graduation ceremonies and remarked "Young man, I knew you could do it" which pleased me so much despite the fact that there were many days of doubt in my mind. My professors would call me into their offices before final exams to ask if I was prepared. I answered, "Sir, I hope I am."

Sometimes they made suggestions about preparation that proved very helpful. All this, because the professors saw me everywhere being occupied by my heavy job schedule.

Actually, it was not really that hard when I considered the alternatives, which did not appeal to me at all!

All these jobs not only kept me in college, but I learned a lot about management, record keeping and time use. Most of the students were from affluent families, but the college provided great help for those in the minority who had to work. At one time, according to the secretary to president, I had worked at more jobs than any students she knew of during some three decades and recorded this in her diary. My classmates were always supportive and the distinguished faculty were so very encouraging and, most of all, fed my curiosity even more as related to history, English, math and classical history and music. Unlike Harvard and Yale, located at large cities, Dartmouth is isolated in the New Hampshire mountains and as a result, we were dependent upon each other for nearly all activities. The campus is striking, the buildings are mostly colonial style and Hanover, New Hampshire is Dartmouth. How lucky I was, to be admitted to this great institution.

My Introduction to General George S. Patton Jr.

While I was a senior at Dartmouth College in 1940, I received a letter from President Roosevelt. The letter stated in part, "Welcome to the Army." My national

1944 General George S. Patton with author.

draft number was 55. I applied for a deferment so I could graduate, which was granted. But, after I graduated I was called into service. My assignment was to report to the Second Armored Division at Fort Benning, Georgia. My first night there, was very forgettable to be sure. First, when I went through the chow line, the cook piled slop into my mess kit - one thing after another. The dessert was lost in the mess. I went to the end of the line and dumped my dinner in the nearest garbage can and went to the PX to buy some candy. As I opened the door a burly sergeant who smelled of beer hawked up a mouthful of spit on my new Army tie. "This is going to be a bummer," I mused. However, things did improve a little each day and I became adjusted to the heavy rigors of training.

One day as we trained, a young brigadier general came into our area. He was wearing a highly polished helmet liner. This was the first time I ever heard or saw General Patton, who later became commander of the First Armored Corps and then commanding general of the U.S. Third Army in Europe.

I knew nothing of Patton's fiery language and stern training methods but, before long, I knew I was serving under a very unusual personality. One day, I was assigned to put on a skit with three other soldiers that was to take place in a giant amphitheater seating most of the 16,000 troops in the Division.

Patton's favorite remarks about fighting the Germans was, "grab em by the nose and kick em in the ass." Our skit was to amplify that statement. I nearly died when we got up on the stage to do our skit where I saw Patton sitting in the first row glaring at us.We put on the skit and I looked over where he was sitting expecting the worst. Instead, he slapped his knees and burst out laughing.

Private Jimmy O'Rear

In 1942 I was sent to the "Hell on Wheels" Second Armored Division at Fort Benning, Georgia. There, I joined with the brand new drafted recruits and the tough, hard drinking regulars who spent most of their adult lives in the Army. The new guys were not at all welcome by the old timers. They sensed, I think, that we were a threat to them and their careers. They were right, it didn't take many months before many of them were replaced as corporals and sergeants. The irony of the situation was that we did not ask to be in the Army and they depended upon the Army for their existence. On Saturday nights they would gamble and get smashed. They lost their stripes. It happened time and time again.

At first I really disliked the old timers. Later I felt sorry for them and their plight in trying to cope with the better educated newcomers. I often felt that this situation could make a great novel.

As a private in the 41st Armored Infantry Regiment, I befriended another private who could not make up his bed properly, couldn't manage long marches and couldn't assemble and disassemble his rifle. His name was Jimmy O'Rear. He had been a promising young Broadway actor before being drafted. None would have anything to do with him. But, I liked him and helped steer him through Army rigors.

I was the only friend Jimmy had because of his military inability. He had a great future on the stage but none in the Army. He did write a play and asked me to be one of the actors. I was as bad an actor as he was a soldier.

One day, on a Saturday afternoon, a car full of pretty girls showed up at our company area. One of them asked me if Jimmy O'Rear was in the area. I told her I would find him. The girls were from the Junior League and were involved in the theater in Columbus. They had been tipped off by friends in New York that Jimmy was in our division at Fort Benning. They invited him to go back to Columbus for a party that was put on by a daughter whose father was the head of Coca Cola there. Jimmy accepted with the condition that he could bring me along.

The look of the men who had avoided Jimmy was one to behold! The guys would have given anything to get in on the act, but they were shut out because of their treatment of him all the weeks before. After that, the girls came to pick us up every Saturday. The hostess was, as mentioned, very affluent and her father's mansion included a swimming pool, rec room and unlimited food and cokes.

When I befriended Jimmy, I had no idea what the outcome would be but I did enjoy all the advantages he alone was responsible for. A good friend meant good times.

The nearest town was Columbus, Georgia. There was nothing there to do and far too many soldiers there with weekend time on their hands. We had to manage in other ways in our free time. I decided to look for an empty building and to establish a library and a music room. Without getting permission, I located a small unused building and got some help from many buddies to include painting the interior. I collected books from every possible source. Then I went into town and bought a record player and mostly classical records. Soon, we had begun to attract the new recruits. One day, my commanding office, Colonel Paul Newgarden, came into the building along with two generals. Evidently, he was told about our "rec" hall. I expected the worst, since I had not received permission to use the building.

Instead, he seemed impressed with our efforts and congratulated us. He already knew my name from a previous incident. One day, a month earlier, I was told to report to a lieutenant at a specified area. While waiting there for some time for the lieutenant, who did not show, I decided to organize the group of about 30 men and marched them to our intended destination. On the way, we passed Colonel Newgarden. I saluted him and kept going. The same afternoon I was told to report to him. "I'm in deep trouble," I thought as I went to his office.

When I reported to him, he said, "Private Nichols," what were you doing marching those troops this afternoon?" I replied, "Sir, there was no one to lead us, so I thought we should report as directed." He looked at me for some time and then questioned me about my background. "Why didn't you join the ROTC," he asked. I told him that, at Dartmouth, there was no ROTC. We talked for sometime and he dismissed me. Colonel Newgarden was a young and tough West Pointer with a great future. We always thought of him as a nearly cloned General Patton. Behind his back, the troops called him "Pistol Paul."

My first pay for the month was $21 (less deductions it came to less than $10), so when Colonel Newgarden made me a corporal, my pay skyrocketed to $47 and another promotion to sergeant made me even richer at $68 per month. Among other things, Colonel Newgarden asked that I start a regimental newspaper, which I did. The colonel was like a father to me. And, once again, I seemed to be at the right place at the right time. Another "door of opportunity." By the end of that year, Colonel Newgarden suggested that I apply for Officer's Candidate School and I did. As a result, I was sent to Fort Knox for training. I graduated in the fifth class and was assigned to the armor branch and to the "Spearhead" Third Armored Division at Camp Polk, Louisiana.

At Camp Polk, our Division Commander was Major General Walton Walker. (He later led the 20th Corps on a rampage across France after the Normandy breakout). He was quiet, easy to talk to, and he looked like New York mayor at the time, Fiorello La Guardia. We called him "Fiorello." He was an outstanding commander in Europe later and probably Patton's best!

Camp Polk was a mud hole when I reported there. I was assigned as a tank company commander in the 33rd Armored Regiment. By spring, we were ordered to the desert training center near Indio, California and 75 trains were assembled. We loaded our tanks on the flat cars along with our equipment. Each train carried one tank company, or other company units. Our four day train trip was uneventful and in some respect, it was one of the best trips by rail I ever experienced. The weather was good, the pullman diner served up excellent food and our expectations were great. On the final day, the train stopped in the middle of the desert. "Where are we?" I asked the conductor. He responded, "Lieutenant, you are here." I looked out the window at the endless sand. "This is where you get off," he added. We unloaded our tanks and gear and drove a few miles to our new camp. There was no electricity, no buildings, nothing, except a long road made by the bulldozers. We set up camp with our tents and proceeded with our training. Temperatures were in the 100 plus degrees daily. Yellow jaundice was a threat because of the excessive heat and it was an experience not easily to be forgotten. But, it was a very healthy existence. No fatty foods, plenty of exercise (before 10 a.m.) and long maneuvers across the great expanse of the Mojave Desert. It was so hot, that, at night when we showered in 80 degree temperature it seemed cold. I remember at night in my wall tent sleeping on a cot that a cool, almost perfumed air wafted across the desert floor. When I awoke, my khaki shirt was nearly white from the days perspiration and from the daily salt tablets we had to take.

I lost 15 pounds and was hard as a rock; I had never felt better in my life. The air was pure and the food was fat free (mostly canned rations). We had plenty of water and on weekends, if we were lucky, we could hitch a ride to Palm Springs, about 50 miles east. Palm Springs was like paradise to us.

One day I was assigned to lead the Third Armored "Spearhead" Division and its 16,000 troops as reconnaissance officer on a six day maneuver across the hot sands of the desert. Though I did not know it at the time, our division and two infantry divisions were testing a theory new to U.S. military tactics. We were in fact, a three division blitz force. A tactic that successfully prevailed throughout the war in Europe.

This evolved as result of the maneuvers in Louisiana where tank and infantry divisions fought separately. In Louisiana, the Second Armored Division was virtually "wiped out" even though Patton's outfit in a daring raid, captured Shreveport, but in the process was ruled defeated because it had smashed its way through heavily defended enemy territory without substantive support on its flanks and rear. Thus, was born the new concept of three division attacks. In open rugged terrain, the tank division led followed by two infantry divisions. In urban areas, the infantry led, clearing the way for the tanks to follow. That's what we were doing in the desert. Proving the worth of the three pronged divisions attack.

On our six day maneuver, I led the division using my compass. There were no road signs, no distin-

Author holds a tank shell at Fort Knox training center.

guishing points except mountain ranges and the trick was to get the division back to the starting point. This was easy, I reversed the compass and as a result, we arrived on the sixth day less than 100 yards from our desert camp much to my great relief.

On another maneuver of several days, my tank company was leading the division during truly oppressive heat when all of a sudden, my tank suffered a "vapor lock." As we sat helpless in the burning sand, the entire division passed us by. For some reason, I kept a jeep with us, which turned out to be very important. By the way, vapor lock occurs when the heat becomes so intense that gasoline cannot get through to the engine. This situation occurred many times. I was not too concerned until the second day. We sat there in the middle of nowhere. There was no sound except for an occasional desert jack rabbit that circled around us before taking off.

We were getting dangerously short of water and the tank was like an oven inside and out. If you touched the turret you had a burned hand. I rationed out water to my tank crew and the jeep driver carefully, not knowing how long we would be stranded. On the third day, I took the jeep to search for other units that might be in the vicinity. After a couple of hours, I found a small radio unit camp and persuaded them to give me a jerry can of water and some rations. When I got back to our tank, I found two of the crew in bad shape. Though we had a radio, we could not raise a response because of its short range.

On the fourth day we really became alarmed, but finally a small army plane flew over us and dropped a message telling us not to worry, that help would be on its way. Finally we were rescued, when a unit appeared and cleared the vapor lock allowing us to return to base. It doesn't sound like a big deal, but you have to realize the danger at hand.

Another time, while leading a reconnaissance unit, I decided to ride the motorcycle at the head of our column. It was about 100 degrees and the Army motorcycle was big and difficult to ride on the soft desert sand.

The minute I started out, was the minute that I realized how stupid I was. Yet, I could not stop and admit my lack of sense and had to go on. I knew my troops were wondering how long this novice cyclist would last. I could not admit defeat, no matter how much my arms ached from controlling the steering wheel in the sand. Then, to top it off, I ran over a big desert rattlesnake. Lucky that I was going fast. Finally after nearly two hours, I stopped the column and returned to my tank which seemed like riding in a limousine. So much for motorcycles for me.

The officer who trained us had come from the African desert warfare and said that the Mojave Desert was far hotter than in North Africa. That didn't surprise me one bit. Our time in the desert was one we will never forget. Yet, after losing 10 pounds, I was in the best physical shape of my life. One could not survive in the desert without salt pills. I made great friends and despite problems as mentioned, I was glad to have that desert experience.

My regimental commander sent me to Fort Knox, Kentucky to attend an advanced tank company course in November of that year and as it turned out, it was my last assignment in the great Third Division.

While at Fort Knox and in the middle of my class, the Third Armored was sent to the east coast and boarded troop ships for Europe. I was stranded at Fort Knox. When I graduated with honor from the course, I was called to the Fort Knox

Commandant's office. "Would you be interested in the preparation of tank warfare manuals"? he offered. "Yes sir," I answered, not having the benefit of a better offer. As a result, I was assigned to professional writers. My job in this situation in the middle of the desert for days to was to insure accuracy in the training manuals. I found this project very interesting. My previous experience, though not that great, helped me in my job and I was pleased that I had helped provide manuals for armored warfare for all tankers.

My next assignment was to work with Hollywood scenario writers at Fort Knox in the preparation of armored training manuals which was even more interesting. My partner was very talented. When the projects titled "Tank Companies and Tank Battalions in Attack" scenarios were completed, I was sent to the Pentagon with the results. After two days, the project was approved and my next assignment was to take the project to Warner Brothers in Hollywood and oversee the film for military accuracy. I was billeted in a hotel for nearly a year.

Everything went well on the films progress except for one major glitch. The scenario called for a scene that showed a tank company attacking a German position. After searching for hours, the director found what he considered the perfect setting. Five tanks were placed on top of a hill while the other tanks were to circle around and attack from the rear. The director waited until the sun was behind the tanks and proceeded to film the scene.

I objected strongly. "You can't do this scene this way," I told him. "Why not," he growled. "Because," I said, "those five tanks on top of the hill would be perfect targets for the German guns below to knock them off, one by one." He decided to continue filming anyway. My only recourse was to walk off the set and report back to my superior. After explaining the situation, I was told I did the right thing. This was at Warner Brothers Studio. Relations between the director and me sharply declined after that incident, but in the end, he understood why that scene would not be accepted by the Pentagon. We often could not go on location because of heavy rains, so I wandered around the studio watching other movies being made. One was *Destination Tokyo*. It was a submarine film about a U.S. sub sneaking under the harbor mats to shell Tokyo. Cary Grant was the star of the movie. When I saw the film later, I couldn't believe how realistic it was considering that it was filmed inside the studio with great special effects to include rear screening process that provided the waves, etc. I also made friends with George Pal who was filming the *Attack* series in stop motion process. It was very slow and extremely painstaking in order to produce the desired results. George asked me to contact him after I got out of the Army with a job offer. However, it was three years later and I lost interest in Hollywood and instead began a career in New York City. The war stripped most of the men in Hollywood so that those of us from the Army, Air Force, Navy and Marines assigned there, had the run of the studios. It was a great experience but, like in Hollywood, had two different worlds. The technical people were 9 to 5 people and very serious about their work. The actor and movie staff were in a different world. Their hours were extended to all hours of the night. It was party, party. We were included in some of these party events but actually it got to be extremely wearing. So, one day, while on assignment in Los Angeles, I met a friend while walking down the street. He was the aide to Colonel Newgarden when I was in the Second Armored Division. "What are you doing here?" he inquired. I told him about the filming. "Did you know," he said "that Colonel Paul Newgarden is now a major general." "No" I responded." We exchanged pleasantries and went our separate ways. As the filming session was about to end, I received a letter from General Newgarden. He stated that his aide told him about our chance meeting in Los Angeles and asked if I would be interested in joining his new command, the 10th Armored "Tiger" Division. I wrote him that yes, I would like to come to his division at Augusta, Georgia. Within three weeks, I was on my way, glad to leave the plush, fast life of Hollywood and all of its superfluous, another world type of life.

Admiral Byrd

During combat nearing the Rhine River, our operations officer, John Sheffield, answered the field phone. The voice on the other end said, "I am Admiral Byrd!" Before he could continue, John snapped, "Yeah, and I am General Patton." They talked further and much to his dismay, John realized his mistake. (Admiral Byrd was on the Western Front overseeing bridging operations at the time). As a red-faced staff officer, John apologized profusely. "Don't give it a thought," the admiral told him. "I can understand why you didn't think an admiral would be here in the trenches."

The 10th Armored Division

During World War II, 16 U.S. Armored Divisions fought on the Western Front. Most of these divisions fought with distinction. (Three of these divisions entered the war during its latter stages. Full combat strength for each division numbered 18,000 troops with three major combat commands and 75 combat companies each with about 250 men.

General George S. Patton Jr. was the first commanding general of the "Hell on Wheels" Second Armored Division. He then commanded the First Armored Corps in the desert and later became Commanding General of the U.S. Third Army in Western Europe.

The 10th Armored spearheaded the U.S. 3rd Army from the Saar River to the Rhine River. Then, the 10th was switched over to General Patch's 7th Army and led the 7th Army to the Austrian border at the end of the war. Since I was a staff officer in the Division Headquarters I am aware of the distinguished record of this crack outfit. (The other Armored Divisions distinguished themselves as well!)

Of the many battles fought by the 10th Armored, two major battles stand out.

First, Combat B Command was a major factor in the Battle of the Bulge in that it was the first major unit to defend the city of Bastogne. Two days later the 101st Airborne Division entered Bastogne just as the German encirclement was completed. Because, General Eisenhower ordered the 10th Armored to be put on the secret list, the Tigers of the 10th never fully received the recognition they so richly deserved. Never the less, their brave combat troops received the Presidential Unit Citation. The two weeks of hell at Bastogne resulted in the defeat of Hitler's plans to capture Antwerp, Belgium and at the same time, split the allied armies as a result of its daring winter offensive. Historians agree that the failure of the German armies to smash through the allied defenders resulted in the shortening of the war by, perhaps, as much as three months. When I conducted 15 European battlefield tours, on 10 of these occasions, we placed nearly 300 roses at the American cemetery at Hamm, Luxembourg.

The other two major combat commanders also fought in the Bulge; 57 German divisions and 59 American divisions participated with very heavy losses on both sides, making this battle the biggest military conflict in American history. It is nearly impossible to describe the horrors of war, battle casualties, freezing weather, constant artillery pounding, tank rampages and death rained on the troops from the sky. It was in the Battle of the Bulge that General Patton achieved the greatest success. This battle resulted in several movies, international attention and, in the end, the concentration camps were emptied of their skin and bones, Jewish prisoners who endured terror, starvation, and atrocities beyond comprehension. The 10th was part of the American forces that rescued inmates of the notorious Dachau concentration camp. To this day, I cannot comprehend what human beings did to other innocent human beings.

The second most important great achievement of the 10th Armored was its success in smashing through the Saar-Mosselle Triangle in a surprise attack. This was the most fortified area on the Western Front and believed to be an impossible task. The key to this attack was to open the Western Front for allied forces to push on to the Rhine.

Later, I learned that one of the top German Field Marshals in his memoirs stated that this breakthrough shortened the war by months and resulted in final victory. The other two reasons were superior U.S. command of the skies and U.S. industry in producing superior military hardware.

Though I selected these two major battles, it should be remembered that the 10th Armored distinguished itself in battle during 1944 and 1945.

One of the interesting aspects of the war was the use of native American Indians communications specialists. Indians were used by other divisions as well. The Marines in the Pacific Theater used Navajo as code talkers, too. In Europe, can you imagine German radio interceptors using their native tongue during combat operations? Of course, we had Indians on the field phones and field radios at both ends of the discussions.

In each case, the talkers words were translated into English at both ends. To my knowledge most Americans today are unaware of this unique form of communications. The enemy was very good at radio interception but there were no German troops who knew the languages of several American native Indian tribes used in combat situations. The end result was important security in field radio transmissions and many victories as well.

The Battle Of The Bulge

Rolling north along the Thionville-Luxembourg highway in the late afternoon, combat vehicles of the 10th Armored Division came to a sudden, grinding stop. The date was December 17, 1944. The night before, General Morris had been alerted to move the division to the north. Unknown to most of us, the Tiger General had already dispatched Colonel Basil G. Thayer, Lieutenant Colonel John W. Sheffield and Major Roger Rawley at 2030 on December 16 to Bastogne to confer with Troy Middleton, commanding general of the VIII Corps. In the early hours of December 17, Thayer returned in time to join the Division which was already on the move. In the meantime, General Morris had hurried, in advance of the 10th Armored, to Bastogne for further orders from General Middleton. With him was Major "Mutt" Jordan, who was later killed in action.

While Tiger troops waited for word from General Morris, as they huddled around their vehicles on the highway, they seemed to sense that "something big" was in the wind. Tension increased to fever pitch by the time Colonel Thayer returned to relay orders to the commanders. Now, everyone learned the truth. As they sped northward, they knew that instead of becoming the "palace guard" in Luxembourg, as many had predicted, the division was to be hurled in the face of a new German winter blitz. Von Runstedt's top field commanders were already sweeping in from the east with a mighty panzer force made up of the Fifth, Sixth and Seventh German Armies-backed up by 10 tank and 14 infantry divisions.

This was the pulverizing enemy attack that created the Bulge. Its purpose was to break through unsuspecting American divisions in the Ardennes and then to proceed westward to capture the important supply points of Liege and Antwerp. Thus, while the 10th Armored was getting its combat operation orders on that fateful day of December 17, Von Runstedt had already launched his devastating panzer-led offensive across a 75-mile front, which at that time was protected only by five United States divisions.

We couldn't know at the time that it was Hitler himself, who, while lying in a hospital bed in August of 1944, after an unsuccessful attempt on his life, had hatched the master plan for the Ardennes Offensive. Though top German generals were opposed to the plan, Hitler ordered that it be carried through. Now the plan was set, and along with it, the fate of the armored Tigers.

The night before, on December 16, while the 10th Armored was licking its wounds and reorganizing after a holding action on the Siegfried Line, the enemy Juggernaut was penetrating the Belgian-Luxembourg borders. It was this grim threat that resulted in the sudden shift of the division to Luxembourg and Bastogne the next day, a day that none of us will ever forget.

Fortunately for the Nazis, the great Blitz was given birth under an all-engulfing fog. As a result, it partially escaped detection by our intelligence and enabled them to crash a mighty mailed fist into the unsuspecting forces defending the 75-mile arc, until now, a stable and relatively quiet front.

White-washed halftrack provides setting for two Tenth Armored doughs as they try on new waterproof boots in northern Luxembourg during the Bulge.

Three Tiger tankers enjoy brief Christmas respite from Battle of the Bulge and open packages from home.

On orders from General Middleton, the 10th Armored was to be sent to a quartering area in the vicinity of Luxembourg upon their arrival. However, this instruction was discarded because of the developing enemy situation. As the division approached that city, General Morris was being briefed by Middleton on the grave situation faced by the Fourth Infantry Division and the Ninth Armored Division on their front east and northeast of Luxembourg city. At the same time, Middleton requested that General Morris go into immediate conference with General Barton and General Leonard of the Fourth and the Ninth. Furthermore, he was asked to assist them with the problems they faced as the Germans threatened to break through their defenses. It was while the Tiger commander was en route to Barton's Headquarters with Lieutenant Colonel Sheffield that he sent orders to Thayer on the Luxembourg highway to lead the 10th Armored to the area between the Fourth Infantry and the Ninth Armored Divisions. When they reached their destination, the leading Tigers rolled headlong into the enemy. Combat Command A, under the brilliant generalship of Edwin W. Piburn, attacked the same day and thus accomplished the magnificent feat of racing 75 miles in a single day and ending it locked in combat. Without stopping, they rammed into a very surprised German attacking force; and while the 10th Armored blasted away at the underbelly of the Bulge, the Seventh Armored Division was holding at the top near St. Vith. Here was the first stopping action being performed by two armored divisions. Each one was miles away when the breakthrough was effected, but because of armor's great mobility, they were able to move directly to the hinges of the Bulge and check the enemy's enlargement of the mouth, and at the same time, to canalize his movement to a relatively narrow front.

When General Morris arrived at the Command Post of the Fourth Infantry Division at Luxembourg, he was grabbed by Major General Barton who, after hugging him said, "Darn it Bill, am I glad to see you." Afterwards, the two generals and Sheffield studied the Fourth Infantry's situation map. The latter described it as "a map that looked like it had a bad case of measles." Virtually every infantry unit was marked by a red circle, indicating the havoc inflicted upon it by the marauding German attack.

Farmed Out

Because the First Army sector was hit hardest by the onrushing Germans, the 10th Armored was "farmed out" at once to that headquarters. For three days, from December 17 to 19, the 10th Armored was placed under the command of Major General Troy Middleton's VIII Corps of the First Army. But on the third day the Third Army left flank was extended to include Luxembourg and part of Belgium. This brought about the quick return of the 10th to General Patton's command. The fiery Patton quickly made General Morris provisional corps commander with the responsibility of protecting the Third Army's right flank. The details of high command conferences to determine the Allied preparations to meet the enemy blitz are revealed by General Morris who described them to the author later. The Division Commander told of a big meeting at Verdun, called by General Eisenhower. In attendance were the Supreme Commander, General Bradley, General Devers, General Patton and other high-ranking American officers. There, it was decided that the Seventh Army would relieve the Third to permit the latter Army to move to the Bulge. After leaving that conference, General Patton called General Morris at Luxembourg and told the Tiger Commander to meet him at XX Corps Headquarters at Thionville at 1700 on December 19. When General Morris arrived there, he found General Patton and General Walker discussing the situation. "Patton was mad as hell," he recalled, "and he was pacing the floor, his hands on his two pistol butts. He turned to me and said, Morris, I'm making you a provisional corps commander. You are in charge of the right flank around Luxembourg until the Headquarters of the XII Corps arrive." Then Patton named the Fourth, Fifth and 80th units included in the provisional corps. In the talk that followed, Patton told how he planned to move Third Army to the Bulge and directed General Morris to hold there until additional troops arrived and to be prepared to counterattack with the corps when directed. At this juncture, Morris inquired, "How long am I expected to hold?" Patton answered, "Four or five days and you had better hold!" After the conference, General Morris returned to Luxembourg to assemble the division commanders now under his jurisdiction. Plans for a counterattack were outlined to them by the Tiger leader and the machinery for coordination was set by the time General Eddy of the XII Corps arrived at noon on December 21. On the next day, another meeting was held by Patton at his Luxembourg Headquarters. Present, in addition to Morris, were Generals Walker, Gay, Eddy, Millikin and several division commanders. This time, Third Army's plan for an immediate counterattack was plotted by the assembled commanders against the face of the German salient. Highlight of the rapid-fire proceedings came when General Patton hurriedly sketched the responsibilities of each of the corps and division commanders and then turned to the entire group and announced grimly, "Now we've got those bastards just where we want them". On December 22, General Morris relinquished his provisional corps command to General Eddy's XII Corps and returned to lead the 10th Armored. On December 23, he was informed by Third Army that the big counterattack plan had been junked and that he was to help strengthen the shoulder of the southern underbelly of the Bulge and hold. A few days later, before departing with the 10th for Metz, General Morris met with General Patton and asked the latter why the counterattack had been canceled. The reason, he was informed, was because of the dangerous situation which had developed at Bastogne. To the very end, Patton insisted that a mistake had been made, holding that the counterattack should have been initiated to "drive those SOBs back to the Rhine."

Critical Operation

Earlier in the blitz when the 10th first reached Luxembourg, General Morris lost no time in organizing the division's fighting power effectively. As has been described, he directed CC A under General Piburn, to attack immediately in northern Luxembourg. Meanwhile, Combat Command B was held in reserve by him. But not for long. Later in the day CC B was ordered on to Merl, a western suburb of the city of Luxembourg, where they bivouacked for the night of December 17. Then in the morning, Colonel William L. Roberts moved his CC B Armoraiders on Bastogne. For the first time since our arrival in Europe, Combat Command B was virtually on its own as circumstances dictated the splitting up of the 10th Armored. Combat Command B was headed for the fiery inferno at Bastogne while Combat Command A and the Reserve Command geared themselves for the flaming battles at the southern hinge of the Bulge. For, as a direct result of the smashing enemy attack over a wide portion of the front, the Tiger Division was soon to play a leading role in one of the most crucial military struggles of all time. And for the first time in its combat operations, the division fought under two distinguished Corps at the same time, as Roberts' Combat Command B functioned under VIII Corps at Bastogne while the remainder of the 10th pushed forward under the XII Corps at the city of Luxembourg.

Slugfest

As described, after racing 75 miles, Combat Command A without pausing, rammed into Von Runstedt's elite troops in the vicinity of Berdorf and Echternach, some 20 miles north of Luxembourg. Here, the enemy spearhead was already choking off isolated pockets of Fourth Infantry doughs and was fanning out over a 30-mile front to menace the city of Luxembourg. To throttle the dangerous enemy threat on the Fourth Infantry's front and to claw Von Runstedt's flank, General Morris directed Combat Command A to counterattack the enemy drive. Brigadier General Edwin W. Piburn, one of the most decorated general officers in the Army, hurled three crack task forces against the enemy blitz in accordance with the Division Commander's order. One of them, Task Force Chamberlain, slammed into the Germans before 1700 on the day of arrival and along with Task Forces Riley and Standish, fought a blistering battle for three crucial days. In the meantime, General Morris received a report that two Nazi divisions were heading for a three-mile gap that separated the Ninth Armored and 28th Infantry Divisions. In desperation, he plugged the gap by sending Lieutenant Colonel Cornelius A. Lichirie's 90th Cavalry Recon Squadron there. Fortunately, the Recon Tigers were not required to hold off the two enemy divisions as German commanders directed them to attack elsewhere. The fighting at Berdorf and Echternach was a slugfest all the way. Always outnumbered but never outfought, the men of the 10th Armored managed to hold the enemy at bay long enough to permit the Third Corps to assemble a powerful attacking force with which to drive the Germans back across the Sauer River line and to rescue marooned elements of the Fourth Infantry Division.

On December 19, Task Force Chamberlain halted the greatest enemy penetration at Mullerthal's "bowling alley," a deep draw which echoed the discordant noise of battle. At the same time, Task Force Riley ran a three-mile gauntlet of fire on three separate occasions to rescue Tiger doughs cut off in Echternach. Task Force Standish, meanwhile, smashed its way to Berdorf, the scene of some of the war's most bitter fighting. The enemy fought with fury at both places, inflicting heavy casualties on the Tigers, but soon had to divert part of its men and machines to the north as a result of the VIII Corps' attack east of Bastogne. A description of the furious battle waged at Berdorf was provided by a United Press war correspondent who related how, "A handful of men from the 10th Armored and Fourth Infantry Divisions halted the Nazi drive toward Luxembourg City for three days during the early stages of Von Runstedt's great counterattack. 250 men, commanded by Captain Steve Lang of the 11th Tank Battalion, 10th Armored Division, beat off attack after attack launched by two German panzer battalions, holding the town of Berdorf during 72 hours of furious fighting in which 350 Germans were killed, and seven enemy tanks knocked out. The greatly outnumbered Americans also destroyed three German half-tracks. The tankers and doughs defending the tiny town lost only four dead, 20 wounded, one tank and four half-tracks.

Hold At All Costs

"The motley unit withdrew from the town in perfect order after they had booby-trapped it. Not a man was hit during the withdrawal which was carried out according to Captain Lang's plans. The stand enabled relief forces of Americans to move up and prevent further German advances. Had there been a break-through at Berdorf, the Nazis would have had a clear road to Luxembourg City.

"The armored units under Lang joined what was left of two companies of the 12th Regiment, Fourth Infantry Division, on December 18 and entered Berdorf. Their orders were to hold the town at all costs.

"During the first night they not only held but actually advanced 350 yards against vastly superior numbers of the enemy. They used explosives to blast their way from building to building.

"One lieutenant among the defenders of Berdorf appeared to have a charmed life. His tank was hit by a bazooka which set his 50 caliber machine gun afire. He rigged up two 30's from a knocked-out tank and kept shooting.

Ammunition Low

"A rifle grenade bounced off a turret and just missed him. Then another bazooka rocket hit his tank, injuring him slightly.

"On the 19th, the Germans attempted to drive into the town from the north and were beaten off by heavy weapons fire. Lang directed artillery fire to beat off three thrusts by German tank columns.

"The Germans mounted an attack in force from the northeast and west on the 21st after laying down a murderous artillery barrage. The fight lasted an hour and a half, but Lang's tankers and infantrymen held firm, and the Nazis again retired. By now the ammunition of the little garrison was low, and there were wounded in urgent need of evacuation. Lang was informed that he was virtually cut off. So the men went back to battling off two more attacks with what ammunition they had. When the supply was just about exhausted a relief train of two M-4s and three half-tracks got through to them. The train that brought in supplies took back the wounded. At 1600 the afternoon of the 21st, Lang received orders to withdraw. He loaded his tanks with 15 infantrymen each-four inside and 11 clinging to the outside. Artillery fire masked the noise of the engines starting. The withdrawal was made without the knowledge of the Germans. The engineers were the last to leave. They set off explosive charges in all vehicles that had to be abandoned."

Men Of Distinction

Every combat veteran knows that absolute coordination and disciplined team-work are necessary to emerge victorious from battle. News accounts of Tiger battles almost always included the tankers and the doughs at the scene of action and right-fully so, but rarely were the exploits and the less-sensational efforts of the remainder of the Tiger Team highlighted in the press. For example, in the United Press story there was no mention made of Private First Class Elmer L. McCann of the 419th Armored Field Artillery in the hard fighting at Berdorf. Yet, the value of his work there can not be overestimated. On December 20, McCann, despite heavy enemy artillery and rocket fire, crawled from his forward observer position, laying wire to the artillery so that effective fire could be placed on the enemy who bad encircled Berdorf. This hazardous effort had to be made to offset radio relay failure from the forward observer position. To make matters worse, the intense enemy fire shattered the wire at three different locations forcing McCann to expose himself to a shrapnel shower again. On December 21, Staff Sergeant Thalen Bowen of the 420th Armored Field Artillery, though beset by enemy sniper fire, risked his life repeatedly as he called for Tiger artillery fire to thwart an enemy counterattack despite the fact that the artillery fire had to be directed practically on top of his position. The end result was translated into extremely valuable time gained by our forces at the expense of a stalled enemy. These are but two descriptions of personal valor by supporting Tigers. They represent the kind of initiative and devotion to a cause that was typical of most of the unheralded Tigers who daily backed up tanker and dough with supplies, medical attention, counterintelligence, air support, ve-hicle maintenance, signal needs, special services, chemical warfare, engineer sup-port and countless other vital services.

Corps Consolidation

By December 21, XII Corps had moved to the city of Luxembourg. There, it assumed control of the Fourth, Fifth and 35th Infantry Divisions plus the 10th Armored Division - less Combat Command B. Also included were the Second Cavalry Group and Combat Command A of the Ninth Armored Division. On the next day our intelligence reported the enemy's probable capabilities. His advance to the west could be continued. He could also attack north and south to expand the shoulders of the salient. Finally, he could commit his reserve armor to the Echternach area to endanger the east flank of First Army's counter-drive. His decision was known almost immediately as pressure on the tigers mounted in the Echternach area.

On December 22, XII Corps prepared an intensive attack in a zone from Ettelbruck to Echternach, then south to Wormeldange which was east of Luxembourg. At this time, Combat Command A was at Imbringen about five miles northeast of Luxembourg. In the meantime, the Reserve Command was en route to Nommern. The foul weather which favored the movement of the German blitz continued its pattern of heavy fog. But on the next day, General Patton's prayer for good weather was answered. Through the Third Army Chaplain, his prayer was issued to the troops. In it he begged. "Almighty and most merciful father, we humbly beseech thee, of thy great goodness, to restrain these immodest rains with which we have to contend. Grant us fair weather for Battle. Graciously harken to us as soldiers who call upon thee that armed with thy power, we may advance from victory to victory, and crush the oppression and wickedness of our enemies and establish Thy justice among men and nations. Amen."

Along with cold and clear weather on December 23, reconnaissance elements of the Division advanced to within a mile of Diekirch as Combat Command A and the Reserve Command prepared to attack in force. On this day, for security reasons, 1,200 fragmentation hand grenades were issued to military police in the rear areas to combat enemy troops believed to have been parachuted behind our lines, including those who had infiltrated our positions in civilian garb. It appeared later that more damage had been done to the morale of front line Tigers, as a result of the wild rumors of spies and saboteurs who were supposedly running loose behind our lines, than the minor success achieved by a few enemy who managed to operate for a short time in our rear areas. The total estimated strength of the enemy opposing the United States Third Army north of the Moselle River was 11 Divisions (about 88,500 German troops). On the day before Christmas, 143 enemy planes bombed and strafed Third Army positions 94 times. But in retaliation, Army's anti-aircraft units shot down 17 of the marauders with an additional six probably destroyed. The same day, December 24, Piburn's Armoraiders captured Mostroff and continued to drive north. Then on Christmas, 202 days after the Allied landings on D-Day, the Tiger commands along with the Fifth Infantry Division pushed their way west of Echternach. Haller and Waldbillig were cleaned out and Belfort was encircled. Further south at

Metz, the Sixth Armored Division, having completed its job of refitting, prepared to move up to the XII Corps zone to relieve the 10th Armored. At 2000, the next day, XX Corps relinquished its control of the Sixth Armored and its attached troops to the XII Corps and in the big switch got back the 10th Armored along with the Division's attached troops. Then, on December 26, after having been relieved by the Sixth Armored, the 10th swung around south to the XX Corps sector where it continued to press the enemy along that Corps front.

On December 28, General Walker's "Ghost Corps" issued the following order to the 90th, 95th, attached troops and 10th Armored:

"Hold present sector to include the Saarlautern bridgehead. On Army's order, advance north to clear enemy from area between Moselle and Saar Rivers. Be prepared to follow XX Corps to the northeast." During the day on December 28, the 10th Armored also managed to improve its defensive positions. Then, on December 31, the division, minus Combat Command B, moved south to Metz for rehabilitation and training, ending the most hotly-contested battle in the division's brief but rugged operational history since its November baptism of fire at the swollen Moselle.

The southern anchor of the great defensive battle waged by Combat Command A and the Reserve Command was secured at last. The period of jabbing and sparring to keep the Germans off balance was over. Now the division readied itself to deliver a solid punch as part of General Patton's great offensive against the Bulge got underway. And, as an act of crowning glory, the 10th Armored Division received the everlasting gratitude of Prince Felix who visited General Morris in Luxembourg. Before the division departed for Metz, the Crown Prince brought to the division the heartfelt thanks of his people and declared that the 10th had saved Luxembourg from certain capture by the Germans as a result of the courage and superior combat shown by the Armoraiders.

While in the process of rest and reorganization at Metz, both Combat Command A and the Reserve Command nevertheless were on call by XX Corps in the event of operational need by General Walker. The Tigers were rewarded with nearly six weeks of rest at Metz partly as a result of the crushing defeat inflicted upon the retreating Germans after the Bulge was deflated by the Allies. During the period from December 26 until February 8, the Tigers had been attached to no less than three different army corps and two armies. Though the 10th moved short distances several times in carrying out assigned missions, no major combat was undertaken. Most of the time was devoted to rest, rehabilitation and re-equipping. In the latter part of January of 1945, small unit training was the order of the day.

Demolition Demons

During the first three days of the division's counter-offensive against the charging enemy, the Ninth Armored Division prepared for the worst and consequently had at hand an extensive plan for prepared demolitions. Combat Command A, now operating in the Ninth's zone, took over part of the demolition responsibility. As a result, Captain Morris Wientraub's Company of the 55th Armored Engineers found themselves engaged in hurried demolition activities. On one occasion, when one of Wientraub's engineer platoons arrived to fix dynamite to a small bridge spanning a stream west of Lorentzweiler, they found that the bridge had been previously destroyed by the retreating enemy. However, in the meantime, a band of hardy Luxembourgers had managed to repair most of the span by the time the engineers appeared on the scene. Wientraub's Tigers immediately set to work with their sticks of dynamite. Finally the civilian repairmen's curiosity got the better of them and they gathered around the engineers to learn what they were doing there. When they saw demolitions being attached to the structure, they dropped their tools and without a word of explanation left the site.

Bombs Away

During the wild battle in Berdorf one of Captain Lang's Tigers found a cache of Schnapps. The stuff tasted so good that he proceeded to liquidate the entire supply. About the time that he had lost touch with the situation the Germans attacked his three-story building. While his platoon fought the infiltrators from room to room, the young Tiger buzzed around in a make-believe world. Soon the Germans worked their way up to the floor beneath him. The shooting finally penetrated his happy mind and he proceeded to lend a hand. Leaning precariously out of a top floor window, he raised his arm back and with mighty heaves, threw grenade after grenade into the room below. With each toss he yelled with great glee, "bombs away." He was untouched throughout the entire melee.

Little Groups Of Yanks Broke Up Big Nazi Push

by Hugh Schuck. War Correspondent, The New York Daily News

"*With the U.S. Third* Army, January 4 - As details of fighting in the early stages of Field Marshal Karl von Runstedt's break through emerge from a shroud of secrecy imposed by disrupted communications and censorship, it becomes more and more apparent that the initial impetus of the German drive was broken by isolated American units which chose to fight to the last cartridge against overwhelming odds.

"It was such a last-ditch fight by Major General Raymond 0. Barton's 4th Infantry Division and part of Major General William H.H. Morris' 10th Armored Division which kept the Germans from capturing the city of Luxembourg and its road network over which Lieutenant General George S. Patton later moved his divisions to launch a counterattack. And it was that kind of American resistance that centered around Berdorf, 17 miles northeast of the city of Luxembourg.

Armor Split Up

"The 10th Armored Division was the first Third Army unit rushed north to help stem the German tide. By forced march the 10th Armored Division reached Luxembourg on December 17, the day after the attack opened. There it was split, one part being scattered to the northeast to bolster various units, while the rest rushed toward Bastogne.

"Incidentally, it was the 10th Armored Division which met the German drive head-on outside Bastogne, threw it back on its heels and saved the city. The 10th Armored repulsed attack after attack in eight hours of continuous battle before the first elements of the 101st Airborne entered the city and joined in its defense. Ironically, the 101st got credit for the defense of Bastogne because censorship permitted it to be mentioned before the 10th Armored Division.

"Berdorf was nearly encircled the morning of December 18 when two platoons of tanks and two of armored infantry from the 10th drove through heavy artillery fire to reinforce two companies of the 12th Infantry Regiment of the 4th Division, which had been holding out there.

"Then for three days this force of about 250 men, commanded by Captain Steve Lang of Chicago, threw back the best the Germans had to offer, killing 350 of the enemy and destroying large numbers of German tanks and armored vehicles, while losing only four dead and one medium tank.

"All during the day of the 18th, Lang attempted to attack, but the German pressure and artillery fire was too heavy. That night he set fire to a house at the edge of town, and the light prevented the Germans from infiltrating in the dark hours. The next morning the Germans attacked with artillery and rockets, but in the face of this Lang managed to advance about 350 yards.

Tank Chief Battered

"That day Lieutenant John F. Gaynor of Ocean Avenue, Freeport, L.I., platoon commander of the llth Tank Battalion, wore most of the fur off his rabbit's foot. His tank was hit by bazooka fire, setting his machine gun ammunition ablaze, and artillery knocked out his last machine gun.

"But under cover of tanks commanded by Sergeant John Shea of 29 Sullivan Place, Bronx, and Sergeant Francis J. Cleary of Roxbury, Massachusetts, Gaynor pulled back and removed machine guns from a knocked-out tank to replace his own.

"No sooner were the guns in place when another bazooka shell struck his turret.

"All that day the Germans attacked and were beaten off. At 4:30 the next morning the Germans massed for a surprise attack. Three times they tried. Three times they were pushed back.

"Later that morning the Germans struck northeast and west under heavy artillery fire. For an hour and a half the defenders beat back the Germans, and then just as American ammunition was running low the enemy pulled back to reform.

Half-tracks Come Through

"When Lang called back for supplies and ambulances to evacuate his wounded he was told he had been cut off from the rear, but later in the day Sergeant James C. Halligan of Rutherford, New York, broke through with two medium tanks and three half-tracks loaded with supplies. With the half-tracks he evacuated the wounded.

"And at four that afternoon Lang ordered a withdrawal if possible. He divided his tanks, guns and half-tracks into four units which left at eight-minute intervals under cover of artillery fire, which also covered the noise of his retreat.

"He got his entire force out of town without the Germans knowing it, leaving demolitions and mines to delay the enemy further.

Heavy Guns Go To Work

"The Germans didn't discover Berdorf had been evacuated until the next morning, for as soon as Lang had pulled out, the artillery kept pounding it for hours.

"By the next morning, however, other American units had dug in on high areas back of the town, further blocking the Germans.

"The defense of Berdorf and Echternach, three miles to the southeast, by the 12th Regiment of the 4th Infantry Division, stopped the left flank of von Runstedt's drive, preventing him from swinging south and grabbing the rich prize of the city of Luxembourg before stronger units could be thrown into line."

Luxembourg

31 December 1944
TO: Officers and Enlisted Men, 10th Armored Division
"The Division Commander commends the officers and enlisted men of the division on the fine work they did during their recent operations in Luxembourg.

The missions accomplished by the division will have far reaching results.

"During the past year, the division has been successful in every operation in which it has participated. May next year bring us similar success.

Happy New Year
W.H.H. Morris, Jr.
Major General, United States Army
Commanding, 10th Armored Division

28 December 1944
TO: Commanding General, 10th Armored Division
THRU: Commanding General, XII Corps

"1. On 16 December 1944, a general German offensive was launched along the greater portion of the Western Front. This division was in position and holding a front of approximately 33 miles east and north of the city of Luxembourg.

"2. Substantial penetrations were made by the Germans in sectors north of this division, and he sought desperately to expand the shoulders of his penetration to the south. At stake were the city of Luxembourg, Radio Luxembourg and military installations of vital importance.

"3. On 17 December your command was ordered to the support of this general sector. Working closely in conjunction with the 12th Infantry Regiment, holding the northern flank of the 4th Division sector, three task forces of your CCA were committed.

"a. Task Force Riley passed through our lines, contained an enemy force in Scheidgen, and succeeded in supplying one company of the 12th Infantry Regiment isolated in Echternach;

"b. Task Force Standish aided in the defense of Berdorf;

"c. Task Force Chamberlain supported our attack and aided in securing high ground overlooking Mullerthal.

"4. Your immediate and accurate appraisal of the developing enemy intentions, and the complete cooperation tendered by you, together with the vigor with which your troops undertook these missions, contributed ultimately in denying to the enemy any expansion southward of his penetration. Regroupment later of the Allied forces to the north was based upon an extension of the line we had fought for and held.

"5. Major General R.O. Barton, commanding this division during the period

cited, desired that expression be made of his appreciation for the complete cooperation extended, and the outstanding performance given by you and your command.
In transmitting this commendation, I desire to add that I am in full accord with
General Barton's opinion and take this opportunity to concur with his expression of
high regard."

H.W. Blakeley,
Brigadier General,
U.S. Army, Commanding,
4th Infantry Division.

Bloody Bastogne

On December 19, 1944, most of the Western Front was afire. Supplying the
torch was Hitler himself who, in a final desperate gamble, flung virtually all his
remaining military strength against the ever-pressing Allies in the hope of regain-
ing the initiative in the west. A delayed Associated Press communiqué on December 26 spelled out in detail the magnitude of the enemy's great winter blitz which
hit Combat Command B with all its crushing force as it reported that, "Powerful
and aggressive enemy forces composed of elements of eight German Divisions
smashed headlong into Combat Command B of the 10th Armored Division and its
attached units in the early hours of December 19, 1944. The bloody Bastogne epic
rocked the entire world with its ominous outcome, for it was here that the enemy
spearhead struck violently in an effort to capture the important Bastogne road junc-
tion, vital to the success later, of capturing Antwerp, largest supply point for allied
troops on the western front."

Just before noon on December 18, the Tigers of Colonel William L. Roberts' Combat Command B were ordered to assemble at Bastogne. At that time,
while no one could foresee the bloody road ahead, there was ample evidence
that the small Belgian town of Bastogne was to be a key point in the days to
come. And supporting the Tigers' apprehension was the directive issued to
Colonel Roberts by Major General Troy Middleton, commander of the VIII
Corps, which stated, "When your troops arrive in Bastogne, place one third of
your forces each in Noville, Longvilly and Bras." Each of these towns was
situated about seven kilometers distant on key roads, leading from the north,
east, and southeast into Bastogne. The roads were extremely important to the
enemy as avenues of attack for their panzer forces. To block and hold these
roads and to cover the concentration of the 101st Airborne Division in Bastogne
was the man-sized job assumed by Combat Command B.

As yet unopposed by the enemy, the able Roberts brought his Tigers into
Bastogne at nightfall. By midnight of December 18, the Command had taken
positions as ordered. Along the way, they passed many friendly units beaded
for points west. At the same time, Eighth Corps Headquarters was busily evacu-

ating the city. In their hurry, they were forced to abandon considerable equipment. Left behind, too, was the huge American Red Cross supply dump of donut flour which was later issued to appreciative units at Bastogne in lieu of other rations which were to become almost non-existent. During this frenzied activity, CC B, soon to be dubbed "The Stone of Bastogne," quietly established its Headquarters in the Hotel Le Brun, right in the center of Bastogne, a city as yet untouched by battle and heretofore virtually unmentioned in news reports on the war in Europe.

Battle History Revisited

There is a saying, "all is fair in love and war", but the valiant veterans can hardly accept that statement, as least when it relates to the bloody seige at Bastogne, Belgium during 1944 and 1945.

Combat Command B of the Tenth Armored Division with its 5,000 men, 75 tanks, infantry, artillery, engineers and other support units was the first combat force to enter Bastogne as the German tanks and infantry were approaching the city. This began on December 18, 1944 when General Patton ordered the Tenth Armored Division from its position in the area of the Siegfried fortress line. This was 90 miles south of Bastogne. This forced march was the first time a major combat unit travelled from its original position with its 16,000 men straight into combat against panzer 10 divisions and 14 unfantry divisions with virtually no time to prepare for battle. When the tenth Armored passed through Luxembourg, Combat Command A split off to the northeast to the Belgian Ecternaht area while Combat Command B proceeded north to Bastogne.

This series of events placed CCB in Bastogne some 18 hours prior to the arrival of the crack 101st Airborne Division which had been resting in France's champaigne region. In fact the "screaming Eagles" units were playing for the Division's baseball championship. They were rushed by trucks to Bastogne, entering before the encirclement was completed by the enemy.

They arrived at 2:30 pm on December 19th. Incidentally, the Tenth Armored Tigers prevented the germans from capturing Luxembourg for the second time during the war. Near Bastogne, meanwhile, the german commander sent a parlimentarian holding a white flag with an ultimatum calling for the surrender of the American forces, citing that to refuse to surrender, the Americans would be destroyed by overwhelming german troops. At an urgent meeting called by Brigadier General Anthony McAullife, the airborne commander, was attended by Colonel William O. Roberts, the Tenth Armored's CCB commander, there was considerable discussion related to the ultimatums. Colonel Roberts told the author after the Bulge was history, that consideration was given to the possibility of surrender. Col. Roberts told General McAuliffe that, as an expert in perimeter defense he believed that CCB tanks could control the seven roads going into Bastogne and that the 101st Airborne with support of CCB's armored infantry could control the fields and added, "We believed we could block the german advances." More discussion.

General McAuliffe, weary of talk coming from all sides exclaimed, "Aw nuts, what are we going to do?" One of his staff officers broke in, "why not send the parliamentarian back with his damned ultimatum and answer, "nuts". Thus, the one word answer to the ultimatum received world wide attention!

When the German commander (Lt. Gen. Heinich Von Luttwitz) got the ultimatum back with the word "Nuts" as an answer he was

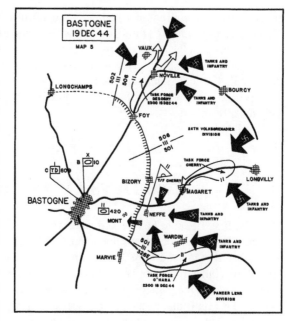

at a total loss to understand what "Nuts" meant. Someone could have told that "Nuts" meant "go to hell"!

Because the Tenth Armored Division was placed on the secret list at that time by Supreme Headquarters and the 101st Airborne was not-the 101st name was allowed to be mentioned by the press corps but the Tenth Armored was not to be mentioned, virtually all the credit went to the paratroopers. This was not resented by the troopers of the Tenth Armored at first but with very few exceptions the blackout of CCB continues to this day causing great anger by the tankers. Some TV accounts, writers and historical videos have partially corrected the battle accounts, but basically historians have been lax in reporting the entire Bloody Bastogne story all these years.

At a ceremonial luncheon in Bastogne in September 1996, The CCB veterans in attendance were awarded Belgian Croix de Guerre medals by the officials of the city. At that time, the author asked retired Colonel Emil Engel (he is a historian and has few equals who knew as much about Bloody Bastogne). My question: "Could the 101st Airborne Division have entered Bastogne when they did, if CCB had not been there 18 hours previously"? His answer? "Absolutely not, because CCB already destroyed the lead german panzer tanks on the main roads and held on until the airborne units arrived".

The city of Bastogne has hosted at ceremonies more than 1, 200 Tenth Armored Veterans and wives during 15 battlefield tours organized and directed by the author during the past four decades.

The final and most important tribute to the CCB Tigers came from the retired American Commander, General Tony McAuliffe as a result of a letter I send to him asking that he be a speaker at one of our annual reunions in Louisville. He replied that because of a conflict in schedule, he regretfully had to decline the invitation. However, he continued "I think it was too bad that the Tenth Armored's CCB never properly received the credit due them for their valiant combat in those dark days at Bastogne". End of Story. Historians please note! If it were not for the Tenth Armored's Combat Command B-no one would have heard of the Bastogne siege because the germans would have raced through this small Belgian town on their way to Antwerp.

Two Days Of White Hell

The first Tigers to be attacked were Major William R. Desobry's Noville defenders. This small but determined force had arrived and assembled at 2300 on December 18. On hand were 30 light and medium tanks of the 3rd Tank Battalion, half of the 20th Armored Infantry Battalion, a platoon from the 55th Armored Engineers and part of the 90th Recon Squadron. Despite the fact that it was dominated by two ridges a half mile away, Noville was on high ground. Upon arrival, Desobry instructed Captain Gordon Geiger of Headquarters Company, 20th Armored Infantry Battalion to set up a perimeter defense of Noville. Anchoring this line were three forward strongpoints 800 yards from the main force, on the roads to Bourcey, Houffalize and Vaux. These were manned by three weakened infantry platoons and tank sections. Though they began to mine the area to support the roadblocks, the engineers had to stop for fear of blowing up stragglers streaming into Noville. A message from Roberts to Desobry instructed the latter to "fill your unit with any stragglers you can lay your hands on." But most of these men were either exhausted or demoralized and could not be utilized by the defending Tigers except for a superbly led infantry platoon of the 9th Armored Division which plugged a hole in the perimeter with excellent results. To prepare for the enemy avalanche, Desobry emptied the streets by moving his vehicles to side roads. Then he told his men to hit the sack for a few hours of sorely needed rest. This command was disregarded as the Tigers watched the lessening flow of stragglers entering the town. At 0430, traffic ceased altogether. Everyone apprehensively waited for the enemy attack that was sure to follow. At 0545, the sound of approaching vehicles alerted the defenders to a "wait and see" preparedness.

Halt!

Then as the vehicles ground to a noisy stop a few feet from the Bourcey roadblock, a Tiger sentry yelled, "Halt!" At this juncture, someone in the lead half track barked commands in German. In the next instant, dozens of hand grenades were hurled into the vehicle by Desobry's men. As they exploded, the screaming of the wounded coincided with their efforts to scramble out of the wrecked track. The remainder of the column hit the ditches to slug it out with the Tigers. The battle was now joined as the leading elements of the German Second Panzer Division crashed into Desobry's outnumbered defenders. In the rear area, Von Luttwitz, Commander of the crack 47th Panzer Corps, bent intently over his battle maps, secure in the knowledge that his panzers were rolling with ease towards Bastogne. Several hours later both he and his panzer commanders were forced to revise their operational timetable as Desobry's fighters grimly threw back the surprised and confused enemy.

As the battle continued in pitch blackness, Sergeant Leon D. Gantt of the 20th Armored Infantry decided to pull his men back about 100 yards when enemy grenades began to **find** their mark.

In the ensuing minutes, the battered Germans swung their remaining half-tracks around and bolted for safety in order to report the unexpected American strongpoint. Then at about 0630, three tanks rumbled up to the Houffalize roadblock guarded by Sergeant Major I. Jones and his Tigers. At a distance of 75 yards, the sergeant triggered a burst of fire over the tank's turret, and he too yelled, "Halt!" He was answered by a shower of 50 caliber machine gun lead which barely missed him. The small arms fire ended abruptly as the enemy tanks opened up with their big guns on the two American tanks which had been supporting the roadblock. Though hit and knocked out by several rounds from the German tanks, the crews of both the Mediums miraculously escaped death. At this point Private John J. Garry of the 20th Armored Infantry crawled into a ditch to aid the wounded tankers and was hit by shrapnel. Meanwhile, the two wrecked Mediums blocked the road, preventing enemy armor from moving forward. But the battle continued as the Tigers fought the enemy in hand-to-hand combat. Finally, the fog, which had been drifting in increased density, forced both sides to withdraw. At 0730 the Houffalize outpost pulled back into Noville. Shortly afterwards, three enemy Mark IVs slipped into the town under cover of the swirling fog. A Tiger Sherman, its armor-piercing shells exhausted, stuck its snout around the corner of a building and opened fire with high explosives. These hits only stymied the enemy for awhile. Finally, two German tanks backed out and disappeared while the third impaled itself on a burning half-track. A sharpshooting armored dough calmly stood in the shadows of a protective doorway and picked off each of the enemy as they bolted out of the stalled tank.

The Tiger outpost at Vaux was not attacked by the Germans, but in accordance with instructions from Major Desobry, it, too, moved back into Noville. During the night of December 18, Captain Geiger had seen to it that all roads leading to Noville were blocked. In addition, he then arranged an infantry screen in an arc just beyond the buildings, and placed three Tiger Mediums to guard the southern and western approaches to Noville. Finally, Geiger utilized a 57mm and a 75mm assault gun to cover the outposts at Bourcey, Houffalize and Vaux roads. When the two outposts moved into the defensive arc, the Germans took advantage of the enveloping fog and moved their tanks up on the road **to** fire round after round directly into the town. Fortunately, no one was hurt, though the enemy tanks got three half-tracks and a jeep.

At 0830 on December 19, two enemy Tiger tanks smashed their way to within 60 feet of the Noville Force's machine gun positions, the 57mm gun and a medium tank. Grabbing their bazookas, the machine gunners timed their shots with the two larger weapons, and together they destroyed the charging German tanks. An hour later, the enemy deployed in small groups and tried unsuccessfully to penetrate the perimeter. Among the many Tigers who helped stop the enemy from breaking through the perimeter were Lieutenant Benador and Sergeant John P. Griffin. They manned the Tigers' 57mm anti-tank guns and, along with their crews, blasted away at the small German groups from the high ground at Noville with telling effect.

Fog Lifts

Suddenly the fog lifted. At that moment the Noville garrison saw before it a terrifying spectacle. On every flank except the rear, German tanks were pushing towards Noville. Before them was an entire German armored division! Too busy to give up in the face of these fantastic odds, Major Desobry, Captain "Bud" Billet, Captain Geiger and other Tiger commanders plotted to stop the relentless enemy. As the panzer division pressed forward on December 19, it shelled Noville constantly. Instead of quitting the town, now a mass of flames, the Tiger defenders countered the German drive by firing every available weapon. During the ensuing hour, the wild noise of battle was ear-shattering, as 10th Armored guns dueled with enemy tanks which rolled to within 200 yards of Noville. The 420th Field Artillery Battalion in the meantime slammed away at enemy infantry and armor, loosing its big projectiles as fast as it could load and fire.

During this melee, a sharpshooting platoon of 609th Tank Destroyers arrived to add its much-needed fire power to Desobry's command. As the fog continued to rise like a great curtain, enemy Mark IVs and Vs were observed scooting across the distant ridge line. Like ducks in a shooting gallery, they were knocked off one by one by the TDs. Altogether, nine were hit. Three of them exploded, and one charged to within a quarter of a mile of the town before it was destroyed. But the most amazing shot of all that morning was by a gunner on a 90th Recon armored car. With only a 37mm gun, he knocked out a big enemy Panther tank. Later, two more German tanks tried to crash through the perimeter. One was eliminated by a direct hit from the 105mm assault gun and the other was destroyed 75 yards away from one of our Mediums. Hidden in a draw were four other enemy tanks. As one of them made the mistake of lumbering up on the road, it was hit by a tank destroyer. The three others beat a hasty retreat. To the east, the Second Panzer Division lost three more tanks to Tiger accuracy. Behind these tanks were sizable groups of German infantry who were caught in the open as the fog lifted. As they turned and ran, our machine gun fire cut them down. Though completely outnumbered, our losses were relatively light in comparison with the heavy enemy casualties. The defending 20th Armored Infantry company lost 13 killed, four vehicles destroyed and one tank destroyer wrecked.

By noon the flaming Noville battle had burned itself out and, except for occasional shelling, all was quiet on the defenders' front and flanks. Ordinarily, Desobry would have had great cause to rejoice at the iron-clad defense put up by his men. But despite his severe losses, the enemy now was strongly entrenched behind the three ridges and, with the exception of one approach, could dominate Noville. Worse, his great fire power could level the town from behind the ridges. For this reason, Desobry asked Colonel Roberts for permission to withdraw to Bastogne. The latter, mindful of original instructions from VIII Corps, told the worried Desobry to continue to hold, that replacements were on the way. Earlier, General McAuliffe had heeded Roberts' plea for reinforcements and had dispatched two battalions of the 506th Parachute Regiment. Under the command of Lieutenant Colonel Joseph La Prade, one battalion hurried to Noville while the other race to Foy. Arriving at noon on December 19 with his troopers, La Prade huddled with Desobry at Noville and together, they prepared an attack to seize the high ground. As both Tiger and trooper stalked out in the attack in the late afternoon, they were subjected to intense enemy shelling and in addition, their attack was met head on and stopped in its tracks by an enemy drive which had been planned for the same hour. Before the unsuccessful counterattack was launched, Lieutenant George C. Rice, Battalion S-4 of the 20th Armored Infantry, raced back to Foy for desperately needed ammo for the paratroopers. Loading his jeep with hand grenades and M-1 ammunition, he hurried back to the 506th Battalion and distributed the load to the moving paratroopers. Then he scrambled back to Foy again, and this time he brought back a truckload of ammo which was placed in five separate piles along the road to enable the troopers to grab what they needed as they marched along.

At nightfall, enemy tanks came out from behind the ridges and pushed to within 1500 yards of Noville but were driven back by the Deadeye 609th tank destroyers. Failing again to crash through the perimeter, the Germans instead rained a steady hail of shells on the weary Desobry-La Prade forces. As the two commanders worked over their maps in planning a defense for the night for the town, an 88 hit the front of the command post, killing Colonel La Prade and wounding Major Desobry. Major Charles L. Hustead then took command of 10th Armored forces there and prepared for a night enemy attack he felt was sure to come. Fortunately for all, the anticipated attack never materialized, but fighting continued to rage on the outskirts of the infantry-defended perimeter. Bazooka and small arms fire kept the enemy at bay during the remainder of the night. Again, permission to get out of Noville was denied to the exhausted defenders. This time, General Middleton, VIII Corps commander, insisted that Noville be held, explaining, "If we are to hold Bastogne, you cannot keep falling back." For Major Desobry, the problem of defense was no longer important. When he was removed by the 80th Medical Battalion corpsmen from his command post, he was unconscious. And a few hours later, the field hospital caring for him was overrun, looted and destroyed, and he was taken prisoner by the Germans.

In the two days at Noville, the 10th Armored defenders knocked out a record 31 enemy tanks, repulsed two major German attacks and held at bay an entire panzer division which thought it was opposing a much stronger force. Outnumbered at times by 10-1, the Noville defenders fought with raw courage in the face of almost certain annihilation. Only these men will ever know the punishment those precious hours cost.

The next day, General McAuliffe and Colonel Roberts decided to withdraw the Noville force to the vicinity, of Foy, which was another vital point on the new perimeter. Pressure was such, that by midmorning, the force was almost completely surrounded.

It was necessary now for the force to fight its way out. Valuable assistance was given by concentrated artillery fire along the east side of the retreat road, while an attack was generated by the 506th Airborne Battalion along the west side to relieve pressure. The column was organized, wounded were carefully loaded into the vehicles, supply dumps were blown and in an erratic fog, the movement by the harassed Noville defenders got under way. However, the unit was stopped by the enemy, by breakdowns, shortages of drivers, burning tanks and one snafu after another. At this juncture, two groups were organized. One was commanded by Major Hustead and the other by Captain Billet. These forces, in enveloping movements, propelled themselves into Foy and methodically eradicated the enemy there to permit the remainder of the column to move. Assisting the Noville units at Foy was Battery B of the 796th AAA. This was the only anti-aircraft unit to operate at Bastogne and it was instrumental in helping to free Foy from enemy domination. Commanded by Lieutenant John R. Walker, Jr., the Battery had been ordered to proceed to Noville on December 20 to support Tiger units there. On the way, the Battery was blocked by the Germans at Foy. Here, a Tiger lieutenant delivered a message to Walker which directed the latter to keep going on to Noville. When Walker was apprised of the enemy roadblocks and anti-tank guns confronting him at Foy he objected to the order. The lieutenant at this point, shrugged and said, "Okay, I was told that if you didn't want to, or couldn't proceed, that I am to turn you over to the airborne battalion in the area." By that time, however, the Billet-Hustead forces pushed to Foy and utilized the crack anti-aircraft battery to good advantage in kicking the Germans out of that place so that the remainder of Team Hustead was able to break out of Noville. During the same night, Major Hustead outposted Foy with doughs and the ack ack men. All night long, these Tigers could hear enemy tanks on the move around them but there was no further action there until morning. At that time Lieutenant Walker attempted to return alone to Luxembourg to confer with Lieutenant Colonel Ormand K. Williams, his battalion commander, but found that Bastogne had been surrounded and had to return to Foy.

Team Cherry At Longvilly

While the delaying action was taking place at Noville, Lieutenant Colonel Henry J. Cherry, Commander of the Third Tank Battalion, had proceeded to Longvilly. There he found Combat Command R of the Ninth Armored Division already in position. At 0200, the Task Force Commander proceeded to Bastogne to request permission from Combat Command B to remain in the Longvilly-Magaret area to back up the Ninth Armored unit. In the meantime, Cherry's Tigers, on the road between Longvilly and Magaret on December 19, received word that the Germans had raided Magaret and had sliced in between the main force of the Battalion and its command post. When Cherry attempted to rejoin his command he found that be could not get to them through Magaret and was forced to proceed to Neffe, where he established his Command Post. At 0600 his Recon platoon was attacked by the Germans at an outpost position at the crossroads at Neffe. After a fierce fight, during which the platoon knocked out an enemy tank with a bazooka, three members of the unit made their way to the CP. There, they reported enemy strength in the village to be two tanks and two infantry platoons. Meanwhile, the remainder of the Recon platoon, unable to cope with the strong German attack on the roadblock, was forced to withdraw towards Bastogne. By 1000, four additional enemy tanks, including a Tiger Royal, an armored car and about 100 more infantry entered Neffe from Magaret. It was this enemy force which bore in on Cherry's Headquarters Company Tigers all during the day of December 19. It knocked out a Medium and encircled the Chateau in which the CP was located. The western approach to the building was covered by machine gun and tank fire and enemy infantry worked their way to within five yards of the heavy stone structure only to be cut down by the Armoraiders. Earlier in the morning, a depleted platoon of engineers arrived at the Chateau from Mont and were sent to guard the Chateau from the high ground to the south later in the afternoon. They were never seen again by Cherry's men. At 1430, a platoon of paratroopers from the 101st Airborne arrived to reinforce Cherry's small force but by this time the Chateau was a mass of flames - the result of enemy grenades and high explosive shells. No longer able to hold the old Chateau, Cherry ordered the CP to be moved to Mont, a small town two miles distant. Before he quit the inferno, Cherry radioed CC B: "We're not driven out, we're burned out; we're not withdrawing, we're moving." Dusk was settling as the tiny group of fighters left the Chateau, firing in every direction. Cherry himself emptied two tommy guns en route to the parked vehicles. He was the last to leave and his vehicle was hit a dozen times by enemy fire, wounding two of his men. Later Cherry was awarded the Distinguished Service Cross for his actions at the Neffe Chateau.

The Red Badge Of Courage

While Cherry's Headquarters Company Tigers defended the Chateau, other units of the Team were engaged in blistering combat. Lieutenant Hyduke, who was killed at Bastogne later, arrived in Longvilly at 1920 on December 18. His mission was to locate desirable gun positions before daylight and to hold them at all costs. From midnight on, stragglers from the Ninth Armored and 28th Infantry Divisions passed through Lieutenant Hyduke's position. When questioned as to the situation to the east, the reply was always the same: "Jerries coming - tanks, lots of tanks." Despite constant movement to the rear by broken units of other outfits, Hyduke's Tigers held fast. Soon enemy artillery fire increased in intensity and endangered the column, which could not move off the road due to a steep bank on the left and marshy terrain on the right. Jammed-up vehicles from other units further complicated the situation. To eliminate the congestion, VIII Corps had given permission earlier to CC B to commandeer any withdrawing units. Colonel Cherry was notified of this decision but his force found it virtually impossible to grab up the hurrying stragglers, so great was the panic and utter disorganization of the hard-hit units coming in ever-increasing numbers from the east. The next morning at about 0100 one Medium was destroyed by artillery fire which dropped in at regular intervals. Then at 1300, the Germans bore in on the front and left flanks and disabled a light tank and two half-tracks. Five minutes later, enemy fire got two Mediums which were located about 150 yards in front of the now-burning half-tracks. This attack forced additional friendly units to pull out which only added to the chaos as their vehicles double-banked the column on the road, making movement extremely difficult. Then too, the 40 stragglers picked up by Lieutenant Hyduke, and assigned to guard the left flank, took off, leaving only 23 Tigers of Company C of the 20th Armored Infantry to guard that important flank. Though Hyduke's Armoraiders were subjected to intense enemy artillery, mortar and tank fire, they held their ground until 1330, when Cherry ordered the column on to Magaret. The withdrawal was costly as the unit lost five of its seven light tanks, a recovery vehicle and a tank dozer. In addition, the half tracks in front of the column had to be abandoned, all because of the lack of room to turn and the enemy's strong attack on the flanks. As the unit continued in its efforts to extricate itself, two more Mediums were destroyed by direct anti-tank weapons and our doughs were subjected to heavy machine gun fire. At the edge of town another Medium was cut off from the column and when last seen was fighting off a dismounted enemy attack. The seventh and last Medium received a hit on its tracks and was put out of action. Finally, the remaining two light tanks and the forward observer tank were destroyed by their own crews to keep them from falling into enemy hands. By 1500, the remainder of the column fought its way to the western outskirts of Magaret to join Captain Ryerson's Team there.

Panzers Pounded

When Lieutenant Hyduke became locked in battle with the streaming enemy panzers, Captain Ryerson's Team had been located about two miles east of Magaret and not far behind the former's column. Ryerson got word that the enemy had jammed in behind him and sent a patrol back to Magaret to clean out that place and, at the same time, hold the road open. At 0300 on December 19, this patrol found three enemy tanks and 120 infantry in Magaret, a discovery which helped them decide to get back to Ryerson in a hurry. Then Ryerson notified Cherry who directed him to use his entire Team to push the enemy off the road to Magaret. Turning his Team around, Ryerson headed for the town and immediately was hit hard by enemy artillery. Just east of Magaret, he was stopped by anti-tank, small arms and mortar fire.

The lead tank commanded by Lieutenant Bolden was destroyed and its commander killed. Ryerson sent dismounted infantry in an attempt to knock out the anti-tank gun, but the armored doughs were pushed back by heavy artillery fire coming from Magaret and could not carry out their mission. Then Ryerson deployed his tanks to support the infantry but even they were unable to generate enough power to bull their way into the town. At this juncture, Lieutenant Hyduke and his depleted force joined Ryerson and together with a group of stragglers, the new Team was organized into squads. But Ryerson became enraged when be learned that his force had dwindled to only 40 men, as a result of the quick disappearance of the recently-acquired stragglers. Nevertheless, he formed four squads of infantry and, with tank support, tried to crash into Magaret but again was unsuccessful. After persistent attempts, by nightfall, three buildings in the northeast end of the town were brought under our control and were held for the rest of the night despite pounding from direct enemy tank fire and heavy artillery fire. During that night Ryerson lost three vehicles to the enemy, who used flares to help sight on the tanks and tracks. The remainder of the Team's vehicles were moved out to the edge of the town to avoid further losses. And additional enemy attacks were repelled there with the aid of the 420th Armored Field Artillery Battalion. Just before daybreak, Ryerson brought his vehicles back to Magaret and loaded them with the wounded. Then, in accordance with task force orders, the column moved out at 0730 on December 20. With tanks in the lead and dismounted doughs around them, the shot-up force pushed north along the trail to Bizory. The enemy did not emerge lightly from the Teams' determined stand as it lost 15 tanks, one armored car, two half-tracks, three anti-tank guns, 184 Germans killed and an undetermined number wounded. Our Teams lost 11 Mediums, seven light tanks, 17 half-tracks, one tank dozer and two recovery vehicles. In addition one Tiger officer was killed, one officer and 20 enlisted men wounded and two officers and 44 men were missing. Cherry's Tigers were a tower of strength and fortitude as they held off numerically superior enemy forces to help prevent Bastogne from being captured on December 19. The enemy never penetrated in strength any closer to Bastogne than at Neffe. All during the flaming battles in the enemy's struggle for continued movement west, the Team organization remained intact and communications functioned efficiently despite terrifically heavy pressure.

Enemy Softened

It was not fully known until studies were made after the war, just how enormous was the German strength in front of Cherry's divided forces in front of Magaret. Later, German commanders testified as to the power they had generated there. Cherry, at the Neffe Chateau, was in touch with Ryerson by radio only. Though the Team commander had no force with which to aid Ryerson, his advice and instructions via radio were vitally important to the latter. Actually, the enemy force that struck Ryerson consisted of parts of three enemy divisions. They were the Second Panzer, 26th Volks Grenadier and the Panzer Lehr Divisions. The Second Panzers had to move through

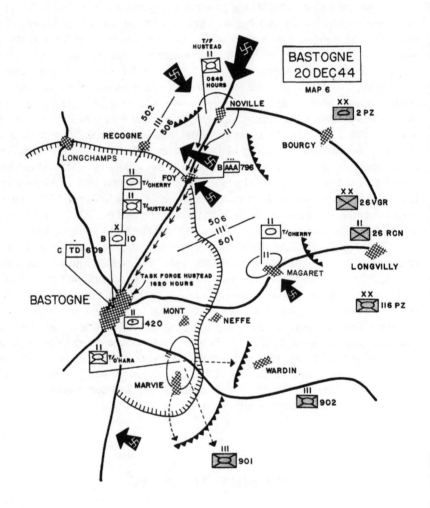

BASTOGNE
20 DEC 44

MAP 6

Tiger units east of Longvilly, and turn north and then west, towards Noville. At the same time, some of their tanks were detached to strike Ryerson's Mediums which had been seen in the haze. Meanwhile, the 26th Volks Grenadiers bore in on Cherry's Tigers who were directly to their front. And, as the Panzer Lehr commander, operating against Wardin, heard the sound of battle he dispatched post haste, part of his panzers to strike Cherry from the southwest. It is difficult to imagine the utter hopelessness of Team Cherry's situation in view of the tremendous forces arrayed against it, plus the factors that the Team was confined to just one road, and to maneuver was out of the question. Yet despite these critical problems, most of Cherry is men were saved along with a few trucks and other vehicles. Later, Colonel Roberts noted that the destruction of Cherry's Team was a minor victory for the Germans in a tactical sense but CC B's Commander reminded the author that, "strategically, Cherry's Armoraiders softened the enemy," and, "more importantly, their stand gained precious time for General McAulliffe's airborne battalions to deploy east of Bastogne." "In fact," he said, "the 501st Infantry was stopping an enemy attack from Magaret on Bastogne at the same time and later that day, it turned back another attack north of Magaret's at Bizory."

Back To Bastogne

Shortly after noon on December 20, Team Ryerson reached Bizory and contacted the 101st Airborne Division units there who were responsible for the defense of that sector. Here the Team's tanks were placed in support of the paratroopers and subsequently knocked out four German tanks which attempted to pierce the perimeter. Hour after hour, they helped to repel numerous enemy attacks. On December 20, in the afternoon, Cherry's Headquarters were ordered to move into Bastogne from Mont. Then, on December 21, Team Ryerson was directed to move into Bastogne. This force was joined by Team Hustead, which had so gallantly defended Noville earlier. To consolidate the battle-decimated units, Colonel Cherry reorganized the Ryerson-Hustead Teams and prepared to lead them as a mobile reserve for the 101st Airborne. His primary mission now was that of counterattacking enemy thrusts directed at Bastogne from any direction. Supporting Task Force Cherry was his Third Tank Battalion minus Company C; the Second Platoon, Troop D, 90th Armored Reconnaissance Battalion; the Third Platoon, Company C, 55th Armored Engineers and Company C, 20th Armored Infantry Battalion. An idea of the fluid battle situation at Bastogne is illustrated by the activities of Captain Ryerson's Tigers there. On December 26 Ryerson, who was killed at Bastogne shortly afterwards, was sent out to plug a gap in the northwest corner of the perimeter. Seizing the initiative, his Team flushed the woods to its immediate front and killed 70 Germans, took seven prisoners, knocked out an enemy tank, four mortars and numerous small arms. Because of men of this caliber, the enemy was unable to make a single penetration of the perimeter. For the Team, the entire period was indescribably difficult. Everyone, including the Airborne Troopers, were continuously subjected to intense artillery fire and the Luftwaffe pounded the encircled forces with nightly strafing and bombardment.

Team O'Hara At
Bras, Wardin And Marvie

During the two-day nightmare, a third Tiger Team, commanded by Lieutenant Colonel James O'Hara, located itself at Bras, just south of Wardin. On December 19 this Force was set to receive an attack. It spent the day repelling small enemy groups and participated in aggressive patrolling against a force which became diverted towards Cherry's men. In addition, O'Hara's fighters occupied Wardin. The strong patrols sent out by O'Hara were successful in keeping the enemy off balance, delaying any major German effort that day. By nightfall, O'Hara was forced back to Marvie to escape a flanking operation by the Germans. At 0645 on December 20, Team O'Hara's roadblock, located about threequarters of a mile east of Marvie on the Wiltz-Bastogne highway, was heavily shelled by the enemy. The enemy's movements could be heard but not seen due to the thick fog. Later in the morning, O'Hara's men detected enemy activities near the roadblock and became more apprehensive as the sound of German armor in the rear grew louder. Shortly after 0900 the fog lifted for a brief moment revealing about a dozen Germans in the act of trying to remove the roadblock. Quick thinking on the part of O'Hara's Tigers resulted in catastrophe for this group as the 420th Armored Field Artillery Battalion was called upon to deliverer a hail of high explosive in their midst. After the Germans were driven off the block they put smoke around it to conceal any further movements on their part. To block any possibility of an enemy infantry attack, Team O'Hara put its assault guns and mortars to work at the roadblock and prevented enemy penetration there. It is very likely that because of the Team's action here, the enemy was forced to direct their attack towards Marvie where a platoon of O'Hara's tanks had taken up defensive positions the previous night. At 1125 on December 20, Team O'Hara's units in Marvie were hit hard by enemy artillery fire. This was followed by an attack of four tanks and six half-tracks. As the 10 enemy vehicles sped towards Marvie they fired round after round into that town and knocked out two of the five light tanks which were no match for the heavy enemy tanks. Request was made by the platoon leader to quit Marvie and it was granted by O'Hara. When the enemy tanks and tracks reached a position about half a mile away from Marvie, O'Hara's Mediums perched on the high ground above the town, opened up and knocked out four of the charging enemy vehicles. The German panzers did not see the Mediums firing at them from the high ground, so intent were they on crashing into Marvie. At about the time the enemy tanks were destroyed, a second wave of half-tracks had closed in to within a few yards of the outlying houses of the town. This time O'Hara's Tigers were powerless to stop them and they smashed into Marvie. Here they were met head on by part of the Second Battalion of the 327th Glider Infantry who routed the Germans after a wild house-to-house fight which ended at about 1300. Later in the day, on December 20, the first snow flurries fell and as the ridges became white and the drifts deeper, the most pressing problem became that of getting the defenders indoors in order to escape the icy blasts of the Ardennes winter. On

December 21, three of O'Hara's tanks, along with airborne infantry support, thwarted another enemy attempt to capture Marvie in the early afternoon. However, this attack was followed by more powerful enemy thrusts during the ensuing three days and the tanker-trooper teams at Marvie were hard put to maintain their hold there. Now O'Hara's losses mounted with each passing day of bitter combat.

Enemy At Bay

At the end of the crucial 24 hour period, the 101st Airborne Division was able to place several battalions on the front. Three were abreast and astride the road west of Neffe. They repulsed two heavy attacks while the other two battalions inched towards Noville.

Thus the Tiger armor, which had stopped the Second Panzer Division at Noville and slowed up parts of three Nazi divisions at Longvilly, had bought, at a high cost, the time needed for the 101st Airborne Division to organize and deploy around- Bastogne. It is likely that without the determined stand taken by the CC B Tigers east of Bastogne, the defense of that city would not have been possible. Subsequent newspaper accounts, movies and magazine articles about the Battle at Bastogne have given little attention to the significance of the Tigers' role, but the men who fell and those who survived are themselves the most eloquent testimony that the first 24 hours were the most punishing and the most crucial of the German winter blitz. Fortunately, too, for the Americans, a local Belgian so exaggerated the strength of Cherry's Team that General Bayerlein, Commander of the Panzer Lehr Division, needlessly slowed down his attack several hours. This slowdown helped to provide the time urgently needed by the Airborne Troopers to get into position for the continued defense of the key Bastogne road net. During those first 24 hours, not only were the Tigers in an extremely critical position, but all the American armies as well. Radio intercept provided the Germans with information that airborne troops were moving to Bastogne. Knowing of no armor movement, they expected to breeze into the city with little resistance. However, the delay at Noville, where the Second Panzer was held up for 36 precious hours, coupled with the effective roadblock at Longvilly, the two repulses at Neffe and the setback at Bizory all contributed to an abrupt halt of the 47th German Panzer Corps. This resulted in a major upset of enemy plans, giving General McAuliffe time enough to bring in his troops and drape them around the Bastogne perimeter.

One Man Show

The writer has described in general the story of Bastogne on December 19 and 20 for Combat Command B. The details of individual heroism could make many volumes if they were available. Fortunately, one such account is at hand. It is the story of a Company B, Third Tank Battalion, gunner. While his account of the two-day action at Noville is undoubtedly extraordinary, it certainly gives adequate insight as to what the situation was like and, most of all, the terrific ordeal that CC B's Tigers underwent during those 48 hours.

ASN 13011643

Private First Class Delmer D. Hildoer, 13011643, was a gunner in a medium tank of B Company, Third Tank Battalion. Along with his company, B Company of the 20th Armored Infantry, a platoon from Troop D of the 90th Recon, a squad from Company C of the 55th Armored Engineers, and a platoon from Company C, 609th Tank Destroyer Battalion, all found themselves under Major William Desobry's command at Noville at midnight on December 18. The description of the events that followed explain why the German attacks at Noville failed and why the Germans thought they were opposing a large and powerful force. This is the account of Tiger Hildoer in his own words. He says: "CC B came into Bastogne on December 18 at 2200 hours without any contact being made with the enemy. Our task force moved out and entered Noville at 2400 without making contact. The town was small and deserted. Our objective was to take the town and set up a road block. This was done. Our lines of defense were approximately 800 yards outside of town on three roads - each road having two tanks and an infantry outpost. The central building in town was the command post. My tank was a command tank with a 538 radio. It was placed against the wall of the CP. Captain Schultz, my CO reported to the CP and was retained there. Upon orders I was to receive a report from each outpost every hour on the hour, which I relayed to the CP. This was done by radio. The time was now 0200, December 19.

All Quiet

"Everything was very quiet. Soon received report that a lone Second Armored tank had come through our outpost. At about 0500 received message that tank column was approaching. Relay message. Answer is to stop column and investigate. Received message that they are firing on us - then silence. Our defense is alerted, and the enemy deploys for attack. Estimated enemy forces are 40 tanks and three infantry companies. Attacked us furiously and wounded become a common sight. Litter bearers are everywhere and the town is under direct artillery fire. Our half-tracks, jeeps and trucks in town become flaming masses. Several buildings are on fire. Due to my unfavorable position to fight, I got an OK from the CP to move to left side of town and away from the direction of attack.

Hell Breaks Loose

"Now the town is between me and the attack. I realize that an attack will come on my side of town so I took up a position between two hay stacks. I have a range of 3,000 yards to the front, rear and left of unobstructed fire. Also have 3,000 yards of the main road under my fire. Things are quiet, so to occupy my time, I map the terrain in my view and fire my 30 caliber at prominent points in the terrain so I have accurate range of all terrain markers on my map. Suddenly, I saw two turrets come up over ridge at about 3,000 yards under glasses. They are M4s of our own but also a Mark VI comes into view so I know they are our tanks being used by the enemy. When they get to about 2500 yards I begin firing. Without a tank commander, I pick my own targets. Luckily, I had the range. Knocked out one of the first two tanks with three shots. While it burned, I fired at the Mark VI. Right off, seven more tanks come into view. I can see ricochets from the 37 on a nearby armored car bounce off the tanks so I know I'm on my own. Still shooting, I think I hit four more but more Tiger tanks keep coming. Hit them numerous times but with no effect. My CP sees that I'm in trouble and sends a 105 over. He fires, but has no effect. Luckily, four Tigers stop in ravine at bottom of our little hill. They turn sideways to us, and the 105 gets them."

Enemy Doughs Hit

Hildoer continues. "During this attack, my bow gunner gets the enemy infantry accompanying the tanks. At 11:15 I observe about 100 enemy infantry break from the woods at my left. Range is 3,000 so I waited until they got to 2,500. Open up on my 50 caliber and stop them cold. The ones that were left run back to the woods, but come out again, only this time there are about 250 of them. While I waited for them to get closer, I fired four rounds of HE into those woods. At 2,000 yards I open up on them but they keep coming. Burned out my barrel so hurriedly changed barrels. A few reach a small ravine 800 yards from me and stop. During the afternoon, four more similar attacks came. I'm short of 50 caliber ammo, so when half-track nearby gets hit, run over and unload all 50 caliber ammo and spare barrels.

Troopers Arrive

"Meanwhile at 1430 a battalion from 101st Airborne pulls into town. I asked the officer who was leading the column what the score was. He says they are going to attack at 1500. At 1445 a heavy barrage comes in and the 101st digs in. They didn't attack while I am with the outfit. Now it gets dark so I moved closer to town. I'm very short on ammo. Captain Schultz comes over from the CP to ask about our ammo and pats us all on the back. He said he saw everything from the CP and was going to recommend us all for some ribbons. He sends the company jeep over for ammo for us. Since everything is quiet, we stow our ammo and eat and I arrange guards for the night. I hope to get some sleep. Skrofichie, my driver, had first watch. Then came Goolkasion, my loader, and my assistant driver, Lester, came up next. He was a new man and I didn't know him. During his watch, he woke me and said tanks were coming. It sounded like a thousand. They seemed to be about 1,000 yards from us when they stopped. I didn't think we would get an attack before morning, but kept my crew alert anyway.

More Lead

"At about 0500 on December 20, the enemy opened up with a concentrated barrage. They were firing directly into the town. Their machine guns filled the air with lead. I moved back to my position of the preceding day. During breaks from the smoke from the burning buildings, I think I got three more tanks and burned out a barrel on my 50 caliber, stopping two infantry attacks. At 1000 during another infantry attack, I burned out my last barrel. I ran to a half-track and got another one. While changing it, an artillery shell exploded on the back deck of my tank. It dazed me and filled my hands with shrapnel. Goolkasion's arm was almost cut off and he was bleeding bad. The 101st had an aid station set up in a building 300 yards away. I asked him if he could make it back alone. I didn't want to leave the tank shorthanded. He said he could, so I watched him walk into the aid station. I wrapped a handkerchief around my hands and pulled to the rear of town until I could get a loader. Radioed the CP for permission, then moved across the road from the aid station. Saw some men to our rear in the glasses. They were the enemy. Got my assistant driver in the turret just in time. Three tanks attacked from our rear and we routed them in nine shots. I was pretty shaky and couldn't judge the range so good. Just about then I got word that an artillery shell hit the CP and killed a colonel and a major from the 101st.

Want To Be A Tanker?

"An enlisted man came by and I asked him if he wanted to be a tanker. I put him in the bow to fire the 30 cal. CP sends me a gunner from a knocked-out tank. I radio the CP that we are surrounded and gave my position. The enemy finds my position and starts shelling us. During the barrage, I saw an infantry attack coming so opened my hatch to fire at them. A shell explodes on our tank and knocks me down. A piece of shrapnel takes my right ear off. I'm bleeding bad, so talked it over with my crew and decided to go to the aid station. I told them I wanted it bandaged up and some sulfa powder on it, then I would come back. I ran to the aid station and got treated. They gave me a shot of morphine and I was a little sick. They wouldn't let me leave the aid station and made me get up on a jeep to be evacuated. The jeep went 10 yards and came under machine gun fire. I grabbed a rifle and hit the ditch. The morphine made me feel like I was drunk. I couldn't see anything, so I jumped up and ran back to my tank. Got back in time to receive a message to retire to Bastogne. It was just 1700. There were two tanks on the road in front of me. Captain Schultz waved me down and got in. I sat on the floor of the turret behind the driver. The captain was now firing the 50 cal. We had to break through small groups of enemy infantry. We came on our other two tanks which had come under fire and were stopped on the road. We went around them. We were then hit twice on the gun shield after going 300 or 400 yards. Luckily, the shells didn't penetrate. The next shot came through the driver's side and killed Skrofichie and the new man from the 101st. I never knew what his name was. Another shot came through and put 15 pieces of shrapnel in my right leg. My gunner and loader, Lester, both were hit in the legs. Captain Schultz wasn't hurt but the tank was burning and as Lester went to get out they shot him in the face. He fell back in. I boosted him out and went out after him. As I got out on the right hand side of the tank, I saw the German tank that hit us. It was about 100 yards away. There were three Germans near the tank and I knew I was going to get it. I grabbed a tommy gun from the side of the tank and shot them before they got me. I jumped up and joined Captain Shultz and the other two on the other side of the tank and we crawled halfway to Bastogne. A jeep came out and picked us up. The captain went to the aid station with us and I never saw him after that. I heard that he was killed a month or two later. At 1800 on December 20, I was evacuated to Luxembourg. I was one of the last out before the town was surrounded. Later I was evacuated to the States."

So ends the story of Private First Class Delmer D. Hildoer. In his case, death took a holiday. Hildoer was in the hospital for 18 long months recovering from his wounds. He was given a new ear and, luckily, his hearing was not impaired. With the exception of shell fragment wounds on his hands and leg, he is good as new again and has re-enlisted in the Army.

Armored-Airborne Partnership

Combat Command B became attached officially to the 101st Airborne Division on December 20. Up to that date, the two forces, though independent, worked together harmoniously. Both General McAuliffe and Colonel Roberts had anticipated a knock-down fight on a linear front. However, without the protection of support on their flanks, the armor and airborne units had to drop back. The new combined mission was to hold, at all costs, the spiderlike network of roads leading into Bastogne, On December 21, McAuliffe returned from Corps Headquarters at Neufchateau armed with fresh intelligence about the enemy blitz. The General conferred with Colonel Roberts and they decided that the Tigers and Troopers would stand fast; there would be no further withdrawal to the west, at least for the time being. As senior commander, McAuliffe had the choice of getting out of the mess (there was still time) or sticking it out. He and his commanders chose to fight to the bitter end, knowing that the Germans would stop at nothing to control the roads for their big push. Thus was the die cast. Only God and courage could help them now.

The Die Is Cast

The battle had developed into a circular action. No longer was this combat with the usual front and rear. Almost at the beginning, the 101st Division's hospital was captured and some of their trains were lost. CC B's trains were sent out on the 21st and with great luck, these trains managed to evade the giant trap. (They returned to Bastogne on January 27, loaded down with new supplies and Christmas-New Year's turkeys for the beleaguered Tigers.)

The fluid battle situation proved to be a tough defense problem even for the battle-experienced Roberts. He told the writer, "I had expected to fight as I had been taught-front, flanks and rear-in other words, a linear battle. But I found that we had to do a circular job. The books never said anything about this type of operation. So we improvised. What a helluva way to fight a war."

Because Von Runstedt's blitz failed east and northeast, his commanders tried a new push from the south, southwest and west. But still they were unable to drive the Americans out. However, in spite of superior forces, their attack washed, like a great wave, around the defenders. And on December 21, Tigers and Troopers were completely encircled. This situation, though anything but funny, caused one airborne staff officer to observe: "Good, now we can attack in any direction."

Stragglers Turn Defenders

On December 18, Colonel Roberts was given Corps permission to commandeer any troops and units withdrawing west. One such unit was Team Pyle of the Ninth Armored. This Team, which had 14 tanks, became the backbone of the Bastogne rear. Almost immediately, it was called upon to repulse a heavy panzer attack which wheeled in from the west where the 420th Armored Field Artillery Battalion found itself in the dangerous position of holding 4,000 yards of front, in addition to providing artillery support for the encircled defenders. The use of Team Pyle and other stray units was of enormous help to Combat Command B. More than 600 infantrymen, seven 155s of the 771st Field Artillery Battalion, Company C of the Ninth Armored Engineers, and the 969th Field Artillery were absorbed. They operated with great effectiveness throughout the duration of the encirclement.

The Big Freeze

December 21 was cold and freezing. The first snowfall forced an immediate change in tank tactics. Until now, the tanks had to stay on the roads to avoid being mired down in the soft ground.

Now, they were no longer bound to the roads. Both the enemy and the Americans had to cope with the snowy weather. Tanks and other vehicles had to be parked under sheets or be whitewashed. The unfortunate Belgians, in addition to other woes, were sheetblitzed before they knew what bad happened.

Inside the 14-mile perimeter, the fighting increased in intensity. Elements of 10 German divisions hammered at the city from every direction. The food supply dwindled to a dangerous low. Only a few gallons of gas remained, and the artillery battalions were down to 11 rounds per gun. On the brighter side of the picture, there was valuable help from a number of units besides the 101st. One of these was the 705th Tank Destroyer Battalion. Its gunners were deadly throughout the terrible days at Bastogne. Commanded by Lieutenant Colonel Templeton, later killed, the 24 tank destroyers established an enviable record of marksmanship. These weapons and CC Bs tanks and tracks were to be found everywhere in the battle-filled perimeter. The thin line of steel and men made up for lack of strength with experience and guts. All types of armor were in great demand in every unit. It was found that a few tanks stationed with the doughs on the line contributed greatly to morale and helped to anchor small groups in their positions, though this is contrary to the teaching that all tanks should be kept in reserve.

Probe, Thrust And Readjust

From December 21 through 23, our troops were subjected to probes and sudden thrusts. Constant readjustments had to he made to counteract the pressing German offense. But on the evening of December 23, a determined enemy attack, launched from the southeast, smashed into Team O'Hara and the 327th Glider Infantry near Marvie. Three main thrusts pushed our lines back and three Nazi tanks clattered right up to the city. These were eventually disposed of, and our forces were able to re-stabilize their positions by morning. How this was done was something of a miracle, considering the overwhelming odds. December 23 was the day our Air Corps was waiting for. It made excellent use of the clear, crisp weather to plaster the

Germans in full force. With new squadrons appearing every 30 minutes, the besieged Tiger Troopers got the kind of support they had prayed for throughout the battle. The panzers took a crushing beating that gave our forces badly needed hours to reorganize.

Ultimatum

Only the day before, ironically, the Germans had delivered an ultimatum to surrender. The ultimatum declared:

December 22, 1944

To the USA Commander of the encircled town of Bastogne. The fortune of war is changing. This time the USA forces in and near Bastogne have been encircled by strong German armored units. More German armored units have crossed the river Ourthe near Ortheville, have taken Marche and reached St. Hubert by passing through Hompre-Sibret-Tillet. Libramont is in German hands.

There is only one possibility to save the encircled USA troops from total annihilation: that is the honorable surrender of the encircled town. In order to think it over, a term of two hours will be granted beginning with the presentation of this note.

If this proposal should be rejected, one German artillery Corps and six heavy AA Battalions are ready to annihilate the USA troops in and near Bastogne. The order for firing will be given immediately after this two hours' term.

All the serious civilian losses caused by this artillery fire would not correspond with the well known American humanity.

The German Commander

Lt Gen Heinrich von Luttwitz

CG of XXXXVII Panzer Corps

Von Luttwitz, Commander of the 47th Panzer Corps, thought he had our troops in the bag. Instead he got "Nuts" for an answer.

The German errand boys who received the message didn't understand what "nuts" meant. So the word was deciphered for them. "Go to hell" was the translation.

During the operation of our much-needed air support, one of the most popular gentlemen to be found was Captain "Ace" Parker. An Air Corps air-ground whiz, he went to work with two VHF radios, supplied by Headquarters Company of CC B. During the three days he operated the sets, he was inundated by helpful hints of "kibitzers." But the value of air support for the defenders was considered by some observers to be equal to that of two divisions. In all, the Air Corps performed a devastating job that has been overlooked by historians. The results were visible immediately. As the P-47s approached, Parker would require half to orbit while the other attacked targets "Ace" knew about. When their ammo was expended, the second flight of '47s had its fun. As the squadrons left for home, they were required to make a reconnaissance circuit to find targets for the next squadrons which came over in 30-minute intervals throughout the day.

An interesting sidelight occurred around "Ace" and his radio tank which had to be roped off eventually to give him operating room and protect him from goggle-eyed kibitzers. On one occasion, Martha Gelhorn, correspondent and ex-wife of Ernest Hemingway, was kibitzing, and "Ace" noticed that the fly boys did not use drawing room language. He tried to shut them up because a lady was present. But Martha stopped him, declaring, "I like that language in times like these."

Dead Give Away

The Germans were caught with their armor down. The clear weather had left their vehicles exposed. Snow tracks of tanks hidden in the woods gave them away. And when ground troops flushed out additional targets, artillery smoke would point them out to the pilots. Yet, in spite of the urgently-needed help from the air, our ground defense was growing weaker by the hour. Our commanders knew only too well that holding out much longer was almost impossible without ammo, gas, food and medical supplies. Most dangerous was the fact that artillery ammunition was nearly exhausted—a tell-tale sign to the Germans of our plight. The shortage became worse as some battalions ran completely out of ammo; others were down to their last few rounds per gun. Small arms ammo was at a premium, too. The airborne troopers were limited to two meals per day and there was grave danger that the food supply would give out completely. While it could, the 420th Field Artillery Battalion provided effective support. Its range of 12,400 yards was far superior to the 4,500 yards of the airborne artillery. The 420th fired in all directions because of its greater range and its ability to quickly lay in any direction. When their high explosive ammunition was exhausted, the cannoneers discovered that it was effective to fire one round of colored smoke to deceive the enemy into believing that an air attack was ordered to follow the smoke marking round. The Germans often took cover, and consequently their attack was stalled as a result of the artillerymen's ruse. The airborne artillery had to be close-up to the line in most cases, which made for a narrow fire sector. However, soon both Tiger and Trooper cannoneers were to be nearly silenced for lack of shells.

The Big Drop

Fortunately, the problem was solved later the same day. The drone of hundreds of approaching C-47s was the answer. For beleaguered Tigers, it was the day of days, as they viewed the beautiful sight of falling colored parachutes, bringing from heaven, supplies to help them hold out. Added drops were made the day before and after Christmas and again on December 27. The 426th got its ammo on the last drop, and it wasn't until CC B's trains rolled in that supply needs were fully met. But the Air had turned the trick. Without it, the situation would have been hopeless. Among other things, even the parachutes were utilized by the improvised hospital for bedding.

In Retrospect

The value of artillery at Bastogne cannot be emphasized too much. For the first several days of the encirclement, the 420th Liaison pilots were the eyes for the entire area. They flew in and out from the outside at high altitudes to escape enemy flak. One of the pilots, Lieutenant Harold Cole of Kansas City, Missouri, was shot down, wounded and captured by a German AAA unit upon whom he was adjusting our fire. Later, the 101st was able to establish an airstrip within the perimeter for use by all planes.

The Woodchoppers

Lovingly referred to as the "Woodchoppers" was B Battery, 796 AAA Battalion Self-Propelled, commanded by Lieutenant John Walker. They did a great deal to augment the fire of the ground weapons during the siege. So powerful were their multiple machine guns, used many times with telling effects, that they stopped one German ground attack after another. As mentioned earlier, this battery earned the respect and confidence of Hustead's men at Foy and at Senochamps on December 20. It was at the latter place that Walker's ack ack men were dubbed "The Woodchoppers" for the spray job they directed at any enemy infantry concentration in the woods there. This was but the first of many such devastating direct fire operations the battery was called upon to deliver in support of the 10th Armored Teams. At Bastogne, Walker's unit provided excellent AA defense each night against marauding enemy bombers and each morning returned to the center of that place to make themselves available for more of their now-famous "spray jobs." On December 29, during a Luftwaffe attack on Bastogne, Walker's advance command post was subjected to a direct hit which killed five men, destroyed his command track and three ammunition trailers. Not to be forgotten, too, were the booming big guns of our 420th Artillery which stopped the enemy cold at crucial stages of the battle. The first big assault on Neffe is a case in point. That attack, as well as the heavy assault on December 23 by the Germans, was smothered. This is ample testimony to the real value of the armored artillerymen. The 18 guns of the 420th Armored Field

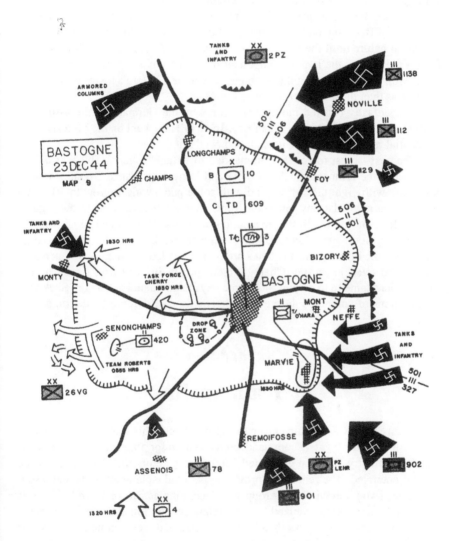

TANKS AND INFANTRY
2PZ

III 1138

NOVILLE

III 112

502
506

III 1129

ARMORED COLUMNS

BASTOGNE
23 DEC 44
MAP 9

LONGCHAMPS

CHAMPS

B 10

C TD 609

FOY

506
501

T/C 3

BIZORY

TANKS AND INFANTRY

1830 HRS

MONTY

TASK FORCE CHERRY
1850 HRS

BASTOGNE

MONT
O'HARA

NEFFE

SENONCHAMPS

420

DROP ZONE

TEAM ROBERTS
0855 HRS

MARVIE

TANKS AND INFANTRY

501
327

XX 26 VG

1830 HRS

REMOIFOSSE

ASSENOIS

78

XX PZ LEHR

III 902

1820 HRS

XX 4

901

Artillery Battalion, commanded by Lieutenant Colonel Barry D. Brown, blasted away day and night against the enemy. With these men and their cannon, American fortunes were considerably enhanced. Colonel Brown was killed in action at Bastogne. He was replaced by Lieutenant Colonel Willis D. Crittenberger Jr. Of Colonel Brown, General Morris said, "The artillery commander performed a superlative job in effectively directing his artillery against the enemy. He was very important in the successful defense of Bastogne."

Because of circumstances, CC B did not operate as a unit after its first deployment east of Bastogne on December 19. During the siege, its operations were defensive in nature until the first week of January of 1945. After the first 24 hours Team O'Hara was the largest component of the Command. After the first day, it successfully held a sector of the perimeter at Marvie. O'Hara's losses were considerably less than those of the other two Teams.

It steadfastly resisted multiple pressures by the Germans While astride the main road during that period. In January, Team O'Hara went on the offensive with substantial results against the now stalled Nazi blitz.

The next largest force was commanded by "Hank" Cherry. This was a force made up of the remnants of the Noville and Longvilly Teams. Organized at the beginning with eight tank crews and with some patchwork, it grew to 10. When pressure was applied to any part of the front, Cherry's reserves were thrown against the invaders. During the Bastogne epic, these Tigers counterattacked no less than seven times. Getting this force back to the center after a successful push was difficult. When the infantry saw the tanks arrive, they welcomed them with open arms and moved over, expecting Cherry's men to remain. The first time Cherry's Armoraiders came in to help, it took three days to get them back again. Such were the problems of command during those hectic days of defense by the rugged Tigers.

Team Snafu

Team Snafu was the name given to a gritty bunch. This was the heterogeneous collection of 600 stragglers commandeered and used for practically every purpose. The 28th Infantry Division evacuated 250 of them before the Command was cut off and encircled. The remainder proved to be a valuable asset in the defense of Bastogne. Two hundred of this group were operating as part of Team Pyle and its 14 tanks. Others were organized to combat any penetration at the many entrances to the city. Some of these men had been cooks, truck drivers, ordnance and repairmen. But their prior calling made little difference. They put up a gallant and forceful fight that contributed so much to the job that had to be done by Combat Command B. Some were already so exhausted at the beginning that they had to be given 48 hours' sleep. Once recharged, they could be used effectively. Team Snafu was also known as the "Fire Brigade." One of the Tiger tank crews who figured prominently in the patched-up band of fighters was commanded by Staff Sergeant Palmero

BASTOGNE
24 DEC 44
MAP 10

TANKS AND INFANTRY
304

TANKS AND INFANTRY

CHAMPS

LONGCHAMPS

502
506

2 PZ

1125

560 VGR

2SS

1130

NOVILLE

112

78   26

FOY

502
327

77

B   10

C   TD   609

506
501

TEAM RYERSON 1000 HRS

TEAM ARNSDORF

TEAM ROBERTS

2000 HRS

SENOCHAMPS

420

ENEMY BOMBERS

0145 HRS

T/C

BIZORY

BASTOGNE

MAGARET

TEAM ARNSDORF FIRE BRIGADE 1336 HRS

MONT   NEFFE

130

TASK FORCE HUSTED 1327 HRS

MARVIE

O'HARA 0100 HRS

501
327

ENEMY TANKS

39

0325 HOURS

SUPPLY DROP 0905 HRS AMMO 1505 HRS

902

901

4   5

PZ LEHR

Domenicona. He, along with Corporal Donald Nichols, loader Sergeant Frank Bullano and driver Sergeant Dean Wagner all contributed greatly to the cause, as did all the other valiant men both within and without the 10th Armored Division. Some of the Bastogne defenders were lucky, while others were less fortunate. One lieutenant and 30 men from the 101st reporting from hospitalization arrived just in time to get themselves surrounded in Bastogne. They attached themselves to the 420th Field Artillery. Within three days, everyone was a battle casualty.

Direct Hit

Casualties and vehicle losses continued to skyrocket. At night the Luftwaffe plastered Bastogne from the air. At 0715, on December 30, Colonel Cherry's Headquarters was hit by two aerial bombs which killed five Tiger officers and buried the entire headquarters personnel. At another time, all the men of another Headquarters Company were killed from a direct hit on their building. An improvised CC B hospital was hit and burned: casualties numbered 22, including a heroic Belgian nurse. The havoc continued until after January 1. At that time, a radar-controlled anti-aircraft battalion was set up in position around Bastogne. With their accurate shooting, the triple A gunners knocked down 10 marauding aircraft the first night. After that, no more sky Nazis were in evidence.

Christmas Eve In Bastogne

On the night before Christmas at CC B's Headquarters, it was reported that the Fourth Armored Division was making excellent progress in its drive to break through the panzer ring of steel around Bastogne. As the Fourth Armored advanced north of Arlon, it looked as though long-awaited relief was at hand. In their great joy, McAuliffe and Roberts shook hands, thinking the worst was over - that the German blitz was a thing of the past. But even at the moment an enemy attack in division strength with tanks was preparing to strike the city from the northwest. So even in their last hour of hope, the Tigers wondered if the Fourth Armored would make it in time. The 15th Panzer Grenadier Division, supported by 18 tanks, made a last do-or-die attempt to capture the city. They attacked about 0300 to avoid air detection and got as far as Hemroulle, a half mile from Division Headquarters in the city. There they were stopped by tanks, TDs and infantry. Cherry's fighters were once again alerted to hop into the flaming battle, but by the time they arrived, there was little to do except mop up the remnants of the German forces. In this battle, a Nazi tank was captured intact and taken south by CC B for training purposes, when it was relieved in January.

Help Arrives At Last

For the Germans, it was the beginning of the end. At exactly 1630 on December 26, the Fourth Armored's CC R, led by Lieutenant Colonel C.R. Abrams, blasted its way into Bastogne. To do this, they had to smash enemy resistance at Assennois, slightly southwest of the city. The Tigers' Christmas present, though a day late, was delivered. The iron ring of German panzers was pierced and the rescue was begun. Aiding the encircled forces were 35 American field artillery battalions which fired 94,230 rounds at the stubborn enemy. Despite the arrival of the Fourth Armored Division though, hard fighting was still required of all units. This was necessary in order to widen the corridor during the ensuing days. The next day, wounded were evacuated and supply trains wheeled in. Along with the supplies came swarms of war correspondents and official observers. The sickening sight of gutted buildings, smashed tanks and vehicles, was mute testimony of the hell that Bastogne had been for eight long days.

Later in the day, General George S. Patton arrived. He was accompanied by Major General Maxwell Taylor, Commander of the 101st. General Taylor was in Washington for conferences when the Bulge attack had begun. For this reason, Brigadier General Anthony McAuliffe became the acting 101st Airborne Division Commander. Still attached to the 101st, CC B was not finished with Bastogne. In the early days of January, Team O'Hara, in cooperation with airborne doughs, made several attacks against the stubborn Germans. O'Hara's Team suffered very heavy losses. Ironically, Combat Command B lost as many Tiger officers and men after January I as they had during the "holidays" at Bastogne. "Hank" Cherry's final effort was a push west through Senonchamps, to help widen the perimeter. Then CC B's Headquarters were finally moved to Petit Rosiers, just southwest. This move was made to make way for fresh troops.

Welcome Relief

Twenty-nine days from the beginning of the German blitz, the Tigers left Bastogne. And most of them would never see Bastogne again. On January 16, CC B, in a raging blizzard, quit Bastogne. Pausing at Metz for only 30 minutes, the command continued onto the area of 15th Corps in the Seventh Army, where replacements filled the badly decimated battalions and where much needed rest was at last granted to Bastogne's defenders, even though they were in XV Corps reserve on a front which expected an enemy drive. In a period of 30 days, Combat Command B had been assigned to the Third, First and Seventh Armies-further testimony to the extreme mobility of armor!

Bastogne Battle Ended

The most spectacular battle of the war was over. More than 56,000 Americans were killed in the enemy's winter blitz. The Germans had thrown 500,000 crack troops and 1,000 tanks into the greatest, and final, blitzkrieg of the war. This German land power, coupled with 800 Luftwaffe planes, struck with lightning speed against thinly-held American lines in the Ardennes. The 101st and the 10th Armored Division took the full force of the Germans' furious assault at Bastogne and at the underbelly of the Bulge, in northern Luxembourg. It is no wonder that our Tiger lines were cut to shreds. The odds were incredibly stacked against the Armoraiders.

Every unit in the area covered itself with glory, and no one division was the whole show. Combat Command B did not win the battle of Bastogne alone. But many military students believe that without our armor, Bastogne would have fallen to the Germans immediately. They would have been free to control the vital highways leading into Bastogne, free to smash their way west to create, perhaps, another "Bastogne" elsewhere in Belgium. The importance of Combat Command B's effort is already a matter of record in military history.

For Combat Command B, the credit due the three task forces of Desobry-Hustead, Cherry and O'Hara cannot fully be measured. When the chips were down, those forces reacted magnificently. Not to be overlooked is the first-rate support received from the sharpshooters of the 705th Tank Destroyer Battalion, the superb 420th Field Artillery, tough Ninth Armored fighters, the Dead-eye 609th Tank Destroyers, the tiny group of stragglers from many other units, and most of all, the help obtained from those rugged paratroopers of the 101st Airborne Division. Of the Troopers, Colonel Roberts had this to say, "Those 101st men were absolutely tops; they were taught to fight surrounded, and few divisions could have accomplished the same success. Their officers and particularly the staff of the division were superior in every respect. They didn't scare easily."

Service Unity

The heat of battle fused Tiger and Trooper into one great fighting machine. Friendships were made during Bastogne that were not forgotten after the war was over. In Nice, France, after V-E Day, a group of Tigers, celebrating peace, managed to get embroiled in a street fight. It was a rip-roaring brawl in which the Tigers were once again outnumbered. Taking a licking from a rival group of soldiers, the wearers of the 10th Armored patch were in trouble. In the meantime, a few Troopers of the 101st happened along. Seeing the Tiger patches, they joined the fray and helped to rout the opposition out of sentimental attachment for their former comrades-in-arms. Perhaps this is what the Department of Defense later had in mind when it called for unity in the services.

Recognition

General George C. Marshall, then Chief of Staff, signed the following Distinguished Unit Citation which was presented to these Combat Command B units: Headquarters and Headquarters Company, Combat Command B; Third Tank Battalion (less C Company); 20th Armored Infantry Battalion (less A Company); 54th Armored Infantry Battalion (less A and C Companies); 420th Armored Field Artillery Battalion; Troop D 90th Cavalry Squadron; Company C, 55th Armored Engineer Battalion; Company C, 21st Tank Battalion; Collecting Section, Company B, 80th Armored Medical Battalion; Company C, 609th Tank Destroyer Battalion (less 1st Platoon, with 2nd Platoon, Reconnaissance Company attached) and Battery B, 796th Anti-aircraft Automatic Weapons Battalion.

The citation read: "Essential to a large-scale breakthrough into Belgium and northern Luxembourg, the enemy attempted to seize the key communications center of Bastogne, Belgium, by attacking constantly and savagely with the best of his armor and infantry. Without benefit of prepared defense, facing overwhelming odds and with limited and fast-dwindling supplies, Combat Command B of the 10th Armored Division maintained a high combat morale and an impenetrable defense despite heavy bombing, intense artillery fire, and constant attacks from infantry and armor on all sides of their completely cut-off and encircled positions. This masterful and grimly determined defense denied the enemy even momentary success in an operation for which he paid dearly in men, material, and eventually, in morale. The outstanding courage, resourcefulness and undaunted determination of this gallant force are in keeping with the highest traditions of the service."

17 January 1945

To: Commanding General, 10th Armored-Division, U.S. Army

1. The undersigned desires to take this means to commend the officers and enlisted men of Combat Command B, 10th Armored Division, for their most excellent work in the defense of Bastogne, Belgium, during the period 19 December 1944 to 17 January 1945.

2. During the period in question this organization was attached to the 101st Airborne Division and took an active part in the historic defense of Bastogne. During a part of the time, the entire garrison was surrounded by the enemy and isolated from contact with friendly troops.

3. This unit, under the command of Colonel W.L. Roberts, U.S. Army, performed an outstanding service. I doubt that service has been rendered by an armored unit in the U.S. Army which can parallel the accomplishment of this splendid group of officers and men.

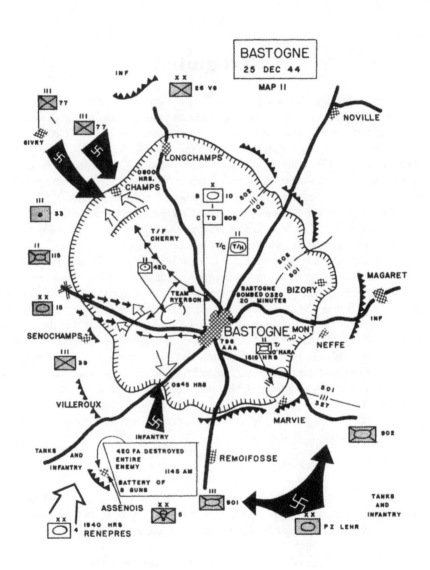

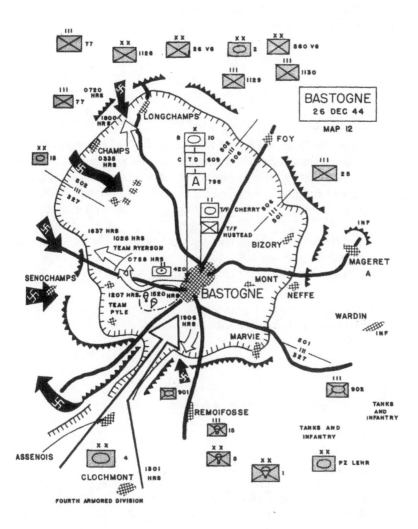

4. While all the officers and men of this command performed a notable service and it would be difficult to single out individual cases, yet I feel that this communication would not be complete without special mention of the unit commanding officer, Colonel William L. Roberts, 13597. The action of an organization typifies the caliber of its commander. The high type of leadership on the part of Colonel Roberts deserves special mention."

Troy H. Middleton
Major General, U.S. Army
Commanding, VIII Corps

20 January 1945
To Commanding General, Officers and Men of the VIII Corps
1. The magnificent tactical skill and hardihood which you and your command displayed in slowing up the German offensive, and the determined valor and tactical prescience which caused you to retain possession of Bastogne, together with your subsequent resumption of a victorious offensive, constitute a truly superb feat of arms.
2. You and the officers and men of your command are hereby highly commended for a superior performance.
3. You will apprise all units concerned of the contents of this letter.

G.S. Patton Jr.
Lieutenant General, U.S. Army Commanding, 3rd Army

Bastogne

24 December 1944
To: The officers and men of CCB, 10 AD
You have been doing a splendid job regardless of conditions. During the freezing weather, whether night or day, with your superb team mates of the 101st Airborne Division, you have stopped numerous strong attacks of seven divisions. You are making history and we are all proud of your exertions. Troops of two armies are battling their way forward in order to defeat the enemy's attack and to relieve Bastogne. They are nearby at this moment and advancing.

The CG 10 AD informed me today that he was proud of his splendid group known as CCB of the 10th Armored Division and that he desired that I extend his Holiday Greetings to you along with mine.

Colonel William L. Roberts
Commanding Officer, CCB

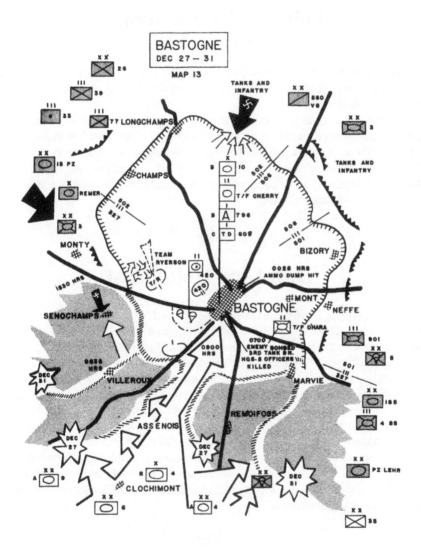

BASTOGNE
DEC 27 – 31

MAP 13

Snafu Becomes Synonym Of Valor In 10th Armored

by James Cannon

With 10th Armored Division, Belgium, Jan. 6: The fortunes of war bilked this armored division out of the full credit it deserves for its valorous part in stemming the Nazi breakthrough.

Junior officers and non-coms who were compelled to abandon the accepted tactics of mechanized warfare in the crazy tides of one of the most important actions of the war threw the book away and "fought guerrilla fashion with tanks."

Not only did they figure prominently in the defense of Bastogne but they also blocked the surprise German counter lunge which started to roll December 16, northeast of the city of Luxembourg.

Thin Line Holds Fast

After traveling 75 miles on the 17th, they flamed into action on the afternoon of the same day to reinforce the Fourth Infantry Division whose thinly-strung line was the only barrier between the enemy and the city of Luxembourg.

By the afternoon of the 18th a task force of the 10th was rolling into Bastogne. It is largely responsible for holding the city until the first element of the 101st Airborne Division arrived on December 19 to make one of the bravest stands in the history of men at war. From the time it went into action until the Fourth Armored Division broke through the ring around the city the 10th fought continually, driving into any section of the area where a fresh break through threatened.

In support of a battalion of the 101st and elements of the Ninth Armored Division, units of the 10th figured in the destruction of a German counterattack southwest of Bastogne. This action has been described by participants as the fiercest battle of the Bastogne defense.

Attacked From Three Sides

Colonel William L. Roberts of the 10th, who directed the defense of Bastogne until the 101st arrived, dispatched units of his outfit north and east of the town to defend the approaches at Noville, Longvilly and Bras. With the 101st they held until December 21, although attacked from three sides. Then they fell back to high ground. At Longvilly the tankers were cut off and surrounded, but shot their way out.

During the fighting around Bertonge the 10th is credited with destroying at least 60 tanks. This does not include armor ruined around Berdorf, Echternach and other places. The 10th retook Waldbilling on December 20 in conjunction with the Ninth. It plugged a big gap with less than a battalion of cavalry reconnaissance troops during the early critical stages, when a breakthrough might have changed the course of the battle.

But what pleased the 10th most was the fact that it took the GI word of despair, snafu, and made it a synonym for gallantry. That was the name the 10th Armored officer gave his task force of clerks, cooks, radio operators and other non-combatants of this division, plus stragglers from other outfits, who inflicted such heavy casualties. It is probably the first time that snafu ever showed up on official papers.

General Charles De Gaulle

During the February 1945 assault on the supposedly impregnable Metz Fortress in France, Patton's superb 10th Armored Division was assigned the task of cutting off German reinforcements behind the Fort. Two infantry divisions attacked frontally while the Armor of the 10th blocked German units trying to support their beleaguered comrades. General Patton stated at the time that the Metz Fortress had never been taken by any military forces for over a thousand years.

General De Gaulle arrived in Metz, France to help celebrate the big victory and at that time, reviewed the Second French Armored Division outside City Hall and in the rain.

My commanding general took three of us to meet the French leader at City Hall. We waited an hour for him to arrive. City Hall was jammed with French officials from all the provinces, waiting to greet their great warrior. French school girls in Provincial costumes lined the great stairway and as De Gaulle strode up the stairs, there was a defeating roar and constant chanting "Vive De Gaulle" "Vive De Gaulle." The general came straight to the small ante room where we were waiting for him and shook hands with each of us. He towered above us all and gave the impression that we were being greeted by an emperor. He said very little. When each of us was introduced, his eyes penetrated right through us. He was grim, he was brief. After some 15 minutes, he abruptly left the room and rapidly descended the staircase to the entrance, where he disappeared from sight. He did not speak to a single French official gathered there to greet him. He rode in like a black knight and departed so fast that the several hundred Frenchmen present were absolutely stunned and, needless to say, they were mad as hell that he ignored them. He was totally independent then, throughout his political career, and as President of the Republic of France.

We often heard the rumor that Charles De Gaulle, as President of the Republic of France, had an intense dislike for General Eisenhower, principally because Eisenhower chose General Giraud of the French army to represent France with the Allied Forces instead of De Gaulle.

And, many felt that from the point of view if you were French - that De Gaulle wisely positioned France in a neutral corner during the post war years when America hardened its attitude towards the Soviets.

In any event, Charles De Gaulle, whatever his so-called anti-American reasons, was a great soldier and is a hero to his countrymen to this day.

H.V. Kaltenborn

During World War II, H.V. Kaltenborn, the NBC war correspondent, visited Berlin before the American entry into that conflict. He was searched and interrogated by the Gestapo and detained at the airport. After a two hour wait, he was denied entry, apparently because he had made disparaging remarks about Hitler. The Gestapo bumped a passenger off the return flight and ordered Kaltenborn to leave at once.

Then, in late 1944, the NBC commentator returned to the Western front.

I received a call from my commanding general, who instructed me to brief and escort Mr. Kaltenborn to our front lines. Kaltenborn was a well known NBC broadcaster at the time, particularly because of his clipped and slightly German accent. He was regarded by some of the other war correspondents as pompous and somewhat of a "stuffed shirt."

I found him to be very determined, businesslike and eager to trespass on German soil once again. I took him to our combat positions near the Saar River and near the

German border. Brigadier General Edwin W. Pilburn, of the 10th Armored Division, Combat Command B, was preparing his forces for a push into Germany. The attack was to take place that afternoon. The target was Merzig - a town of tactical importance, since it overlooked the valley. This is what transpired from that point on.

Kaltenborn: "Captain Nichols, do you know exactly where the German border is?"

Nichols: "Yes, Sir, it is about a mile from here."

Kaltenborn: "Do you think it is dangerous to cross the border for even just a few feet?"

Nichols: "No, there is no danger. I know Captain 'Bud' Billett who commands B Company of the 20th Armored Infantry Battalion. Bud told me his company was in a holding position and little action was taking place except for nightly patrols."

Kaltenborn: "Fine, let's go to that area - I must personally cross that border today."

Nichols: "Well, here we are, about 50 yards across the border on German soil."

Kaltenborn: "Are you sure there are no German troops in this vicinity - it's safe?"

Nichols: "I'm sure your walk across the border will be uneventful."

His feat accomplished, Kaltenborn returned the 50 yards to the border somewhat out of breath and at the same time, jubilant that he had defied Hitler by entering Germany again - and, without a shot being fire! After that dull and uneventful afternoon, I escorted the NBC war correspondent to Luxembourg where he was to deliver his nightly broadcast. Listening to his commentary was an experience I'll never forget.

Among his clipped, war news observations on the broadcast were these comments:

"Today, I went back into Germany. Some five years ago, and two days before this war began, Adolf Hitler sent me out of Germany because I had told the truth about him."

"Today, I went back in with the 10th Armored Division of Patton's Third Army. And, Hitler didn't stop me! I got the feel of his artillery fire, but I also got the feel of the fighting qualities of our combat soldiers who are defeating Hitler's armies."

Had I known the day with him at the Front was going to be so exciting and so dangerous, I might have been scared at the thought of crossing that "fiery" German border with Kaltenborn.

A Night Of Hell

While the 10th Armored Division was spearheading Patton's U.S. Third Army across the Palatinate region in Germany, our division's headquarters was billeted in an abandoned school house overnight.

There was a long road uphill about 2,000 yards to the German positions from our vantage point. We had little sleep for several days, so I took my bedroll to an upper floor of the school house. Laying out on the bedroll on the bare floor, I soon went to sleep.

After a couple of hours had elapsed, I woke up to a thunderous noise of cannon fire, small arms fire and in effect, it seemed that the world was being blown up. I was truly so exhausted that I didn't really care what happened and went back to sleep.

When I woke up at dawn, there was total silence. I thought the Germans had captured the school house and missed me on one of the upper flours. Creeping to a window, I carefully approached the side of the window and peeked down. What I saw led me to believe that this would be the last day of the war for me. Below me was a giant German Tiger tank with its 90 millimeter gun pointed straight up to the window!

Walking away, very quietly, I pick up my gear. I moved very carefully down the hall to the stairs. There was absolutely not a sound anywhere. It crossed my mind that everyone had been killed. Proceeding further downstairs, I came to another hall and cautiously approached a doorway leading to outside the building. When I got there, I heard sounds of men talking. Peeking out the door, I saw to my astonishment, a group of GIs eating breakfast at chow truck. I couldn't believe what I was seeing. I joined the troops.

Then, I found out what all the explosions I heard during the night were. The division ammunition trucks, about 20 of them, were located near the school house. During the night, German gunners had fired several dozen 88s on the pin-pointed truck area. The trucks caught on fire and all the ammunition blew up.

Though it was a night of hell, the consequences were really to my liking.

P.S.: I found out later that the German Tiger Panzer tank I saw had been destroyed earlier.

General Patton's Wartime Speech To His Troops

"We are here," the speaker said, "to listen to the words of a great man. A man who will lead you into whatever you might face with heroism, ability and foresight. A man who has proven himself amid shot and shell."

General Patton arose and strode swiftly to the microphone. The men snapped to their feet and stood silently. Patton surveyed them grimly. "Be seated," the words were not a request but a command. The General's voice arose high and clear.

"Men, this stuff we hear about America wanting to stay out of this war, not wanting to fight, is a lot of bull. Americans love to fight. All real Americans love the sting of battle. Americans love a winner and do not tolerate a loser. Americans despise cowards. Americans play to win all the time. I wouldn't give a hoot in hell for a man who lost and laughed. That's why Americans have never lost, and will never lose a war, for the very thought of losing is hateful to an American."

He paused and looked over the silent crowd. "You are not all going to die. Only two percent of you here will die in a major battle. Death must not be feared. Every man is frightened at first in battle. If he says he isn't, he's a liar. Some men are cowards, yes, but they will fight just the same, or get the hell shamed out of them. Some get over their fright in a few minutes under, some take hours, for some it takes days. The real man never lets the fear of death overpower his honor and his sense of duty. All through your career of Army life, you men have bitched about what you call 'this chicken-@1#@ drilling'. This is all for purpose. Drilling and discipline must be maintained in the Army. If only for one reason: Instant obedience to orders! I don't give a damn for a man who is not always on his toes. You men are veterans or you would not be here. If not, sometime a German will sneak up behind you and beat you to death."

General Patton visits Tenth Armored Headquarters Gen. Mprris - Gen. Prickett, Tenth Armored Commanders 1945.

The men roared. Patton's grim expression did not change. "There are 400 neatly marked graves somewhere in Europe," he roared, "all because ONE MAN went to sleep on his job." He paused, and then grew silent. "But they are German graves," he said softly, "for we caught the bastards asleep!"

The general clenched the microphone tightly, "An Army is a team. lives, sleeps, eats, fights as a team. This individual stuff is a lot of crap. The bilious bastards who wrote that kind of stuff for the *Saturday Evening Post* don't know anymore about real battle than they do about fornicating."

"We have the finest food, the finest equipment, best spirit and men in the world," Patton bellowed. "Why, by God," he thundered, "I actually pity these sons-of-bitches we're in against, by God, I do." The men clapped their hands and howled.

"My men don't surrender," Patton continued. He halted, and the crowd waited. "All the real heroes are not story-book combat fighters, either," he went on. "Every man in the Army plays a vital part. Every little job is essential to the whole scheme. What if every truck driver suddenly decided that he didn't like the whine of those shells and turned yellow and jumped headlong into the ditch? He could say to himself, they won't miss me. What if every man said that? Every man does his job. Every man, every department, every unit is important in the vast scheme of things. The Ordnance men are needed to supply guns, the Quartermaster to bring up the food and clothes for us, for where we are going there isn't a hell of a lot to eat. Every damn last man in the mess hall, even the one who heats the water to keep us from getting diarrhea, has a job to do. Even the Chaplain is important, for if we get killed

"A Promise" Gen. George Patton. Rhine '45.

and he wasn't there to bury us, we'd all go to hell. Each man must not only think of himself but think of his buddy fighting beside him. We don't want cowards in the Army. The brave men will breed more brave men. One of the bravest men I saw was in the African Campaign. The fellow I saw on the top of a telegraph pole in the midst of furious fire. I stopped and asked him what in the hell he was doing up there at this time. He answered, 'fixing the wire, Sir'. 'Isn't it a little unhealthy up there?', I asked. 'Yes sir, but this wire has to be fixed.' There was a real soldier. There was a man who devoted all to his duty, no matter how great the odds, no matter how seemingly insignificant his duty may have seemed at that time."

The general paused, staring challenging out over the silent sea of faces. You could hear a pin drop anywhere on the vast hillside. "Don't forget," Patton barked, "you don't know I'm here." No word of that fact is to be mentioned in any letters. The world is not supposed to know what the hell they did with me. I'm not supposed to be commanding this Army. Let the first bastards to find out be the Germans! Some day I want them to raise up on their hind legs and howl, "It's the Third Army and Patton again."

"We want to get the hell out of here," Patton yelled. "We want to clean the darn thing up. And, then we'll have to take a little jaunt against the Japs and clean their nest out, too."

The crowd laughed and Patton continued quietly, "Sure we all want to go home, we want this thing over with, but you can't win a war laying down. The quickest way to get it over with is to go to the bastards. The quicker they are whipped, the quicker we go home. The shortest way home is through Berlin. There is no such thing as a foxhole war anymore. Foxholes slow up an offensive. KEEP MOVING! We'll win the war, but we'll win it by fighting and showing our guts." He paused and his eagle-eye swept over the crowd.

"There's one great thing you men will be able to say when we go home. You may all thank God for it. Thank God that, years from now when you are sitting around the fire-side with your grandson on your knee and he asks you what you did in the war, you won't have to pause and say, "Why, I shoveled shit in Louisiana."

General Dwight D. Eisenhower
Allied Forces Supreme Commander In World War II

Almost everyone is aware of the problems faced by Eisenhower with General George S. Patton Jr. At that time of the war Patton commanded the U.S. Third Army. What few people know is that Patton got the best of his Supreme Commander at least on one occasion during the big conflict in Europe.

It was on February 27, 1944 when Patton decided on a daring, but very risky, attack through the heavily fortified 19 mile long Saar-Moselle triangle, an area bordered by France, Belgium and Germany. Seven miles of obstacles barred the way to success in the attack. The Saar River, the Moselle River, anti-tank ditches, concrete dragons teeth, pillboxes, artillery and enemy troops were in the way. Patton, who was a stickler for "going by the book" brushed aside tank-infantry tactics as taught by the Armored School at Fort Knox and ordered the crack 10th Armored Division to attack with the intent to capture Trier, the prize of the fortified triangle.

No one in their right mind would order an armored division to attack such a formidable defense and this was in the mind of the German commanders as well.

While all this was taking place, General Eisenhower, looking at the map in the huge war room at SHAEF, apparently decided that Patton might undertake a grandstand play. On March 1st, he sent this message to General Patton. "Don't attempt to capture Trier, it would take at least four divisions and would be too costly."

The message was received on the day the victorious 10th Armored Tigers had captured Trier and had already raised the American flag at their headquarters on the famed Hitler Platz, across from the ancient Roman Porta Negra arch.

Patton was in the 10th Armored Headquarters in Trier when the terse message arrived. He burst into laughter when he read the Supreme Commander's directive. His mood suddenly changed, though, and he dictated the following reply, "We have just captured Trier with one armored division - do you want me to give it back to the bastards!" We were not aware of Ike's reception but one could guess his anger. Yet, he had to be pleased with this dramatic victory, since it opened the way to the Rhine River for Allied units to pour through the gap. This campaign was so daring, that for years, it was a subject of study taught to armored division leaders at Fort Knox.

On March 7, General Eisenhower came to Trier to join in the celebration. He was accompanied by the 20th Corps Commander, General Walton Walker. Patton turned to Walker and blurted, "If it had not been for the 10th Armored Division, I would have relieved you." General Eisenhower then chipped in, "George, if it were not for the 10th Armored, I might have done some relieving myself."

All this seemed in good humor despite Patton disobeying his superior. Few knew about this exchange of words and still fewer knew that if it had been up to Eisenhower, the great successful thrust would not have taken place. As Ike toured the division area, he was hailed as a conquering hero.

General George S. Patton Jr.
U.S. Third Army - Europe
Colorful Anecdotes

In Louisiana on maneuvers with Patton commanding the Second Armored Division, a chaplain who had just joined the division was attempting to put up a small wall tent and needed help. He asked the author, who was nearby, to assist him. Noting that the chaplain was a captain and not entitled to that type of tent, the author told the chaplain he was violating regulations. The chaplain replied, "What's the difference, I'm only a chaplain." While the author was inside the tent holding the main pole for the chaplain, he heard a familiar voice - that of General Patton who was on an inspection tour. Patton growled, "Who in the hell is putting up this damned tent?" The chaplain, unaware of General Patton's reputation, replied, "Why, it's mine, Sir. I'm the chaplain." The General looked at him and bellowed, "I don't give a damn who you are, take down that @#!@ tent now!" During this episode, I remained very quiet inside the tent. After Patton left the area, the I came out and saw a bewildered chaplain with his hands on his hips who exclaimed, "My, he swears a lot, doesn't he!" Three years later in Luxembourg at U.S. Third Army Headquarters, I spent an hour with Patton but at that time failed to tell the General he had been assisting the chaplain inside the tent on that day earlier in Louisiana.

•The Saar-Moselle Triangle was the most heavily fortified area on the Western Front in Europe in World War II. General Eisenhower at Supreme Headquarters noted that Patton's U.S. Third Army was in the vicinity of that area. Fearing Patton might make a grandstand play and attack, he telegraphed the Third Army Commander as follows: Don't attempt to capture Trier (the key to the breakthrough). It would be too costly and would take at least four Divisions." In the meantime, Patton had already successfully rammed the 10th Armored Division through the German fortified area. Later, at 10th Armored Headquarters in Trier, Eisenhower's telegram reached Patton. "Get me a stenographer!," he snapped. Patton then sent this message to the Supreme Commander: "We have just captured Trier with one Armored Division - do you want me to give it back to the bastards?"

•Both the U.S. Third and Seventh armies were racing headlong across the Palatinate area to the Rhine. Patton, Commander of the Third Army, saw an opportunity to cut off and capture 50,000 German troops who, because all bridges were blown, could not retreat further into Germany. He directed the 10th Armored Division to wheel sharply on its right flank, cut across General Patch's U.S. Seventh Army, closed the pocket and hauled in 50,000 bewildered German troops. General Patch was incensed at this tactic and telegraphed Patton "Congratulations, George, you have just surrounded the entire Seventh Army."

•Visiting the 10th Armored's Headquarters area one day, Patton came across a young 10th Armored Tiger in a field hospital. "What happened to you?," Patton kindly inquired. The soldier nervously shifted in his cot and answered, "Why, I've got hives, Sir," Patton laughed and patted him on the head. "Nonsense, he said, "why don't you admit you were shot in the butt?"

•During the same battle our tactical fighter planes could not attack the massed German tank and infantry columns because of an intense fog. Patton summoned his Army Chaplain and explained he wanted a prayer for good weather and then ordered, "It better be a darned good prayer!" This was the result: "Almighty and most merciful Father, we humbly beseech Thee of they great goodness, to restrain these immoderate rains with which we have had to contend. Grant us fair weather for battle. Graciously hearken to us as soldiers who call upon Thee that armed with Thy power, we may advance from victory to victory, and crush the oppression and wickedness of our enemies, and establish Thy justice among men and nations. Amen."

Jack Benny

During the occupation of southern Germany after World War II, the Army Special Services sent several big name entertainers to Garmisch, Southern Bavaria to entertain the occupation forces. I was assigned, among others, to Jack Benny to escort him around the area.

The first thing he told me was, "I am not here to entertain the officers, I'm here for the troops." I replied, "whatever you want to do is okay with me." He then put on a show in the Olympic Stadium that drew several thousand GIs who applauded vigorously during the two hour event. Some of the officers wondered why they didn't get to meet him. I evaded the question by telling them his schedule was so tight, he couldn't cover all the bases. Larry Adler, the famed harmonica virtuoso joined him in the show. Larry had been unfairly caught up in the congressional

Jack Benny and singer Martha Tilton at Garmiseh, Germany at Tenth Armored Division Occupation area. 1945.

witch hunt earlier and had been accused of communist affiliation, but he prevailed. His one request of me was to help find harmonicas. We were able to collect several hundred so that he could hand them out to the troops. I really liked him and really felt he was subjected to unfair treatment. He was a very generous artist and was very much appreciated by the troops.

Another entertainer was singer Martha Tilton whose brother was in the 10th Armored Division Occupation Forces. "Can you help me find my brother," she asked. I told her that we would. When we brought him to her at Division headquarters, she was overjoyed. Their reunion was something to behold!

The Big Wartime Champaign Party

During World War II when I was assigned to the U.S. 3rd Army Press Corps, I was privileged to know many of the top War Correspondents from America and England. Except when I was a censor at the press camp, I was on good terms with these distinguished War Correspondents. When they wrote their daily communiqués, they were required to submit their copies to me. I had a list of words and phrases that could not be included in their copies. When they submitted their news copies, I would cut out all statements as per my no no list with a razor blade. In returning their copy to them, which sometimes looked like a party shredded sheet of paper, they would raise hell with me. "Damn you," they would yell at me and continued their ranting, "You ruined my copy." I replied, "I'm really sorry, but the safety of our troops is a hell of a lot more important than your copies."

We somehow managed to get along despite these flaks. I had a call one day from an Army friend who was at Trier, Germany, the oldest city in Germany (formerly called Treve by the Romans who in their conquest established it as their farthest Roman outpost 2,000 years earlier). Trier also is a site of one of the world's great intact treasures, the Porta Negra Arch (or the Black Gate), which was about 12 stories high and was the centerpiece of the fortified walled city of Trier. I remember too that the Air Force issued strict orders not to bomb the ancient arch. It was the only entrance to the walled city of Trier.

My friend informed me that there was a champaign facility in Trier that was for the most part spared from bombing attacks. He said, "Les, this place is full of fancy champaign. Come on down and load up." This I did, because I had something in mind which was to score points with the War Correspondents. Trier was captured by the 10th Armored Division and was occupying the area at the time. When I arrived there, I climbed down a bomb shattered stairway and saw thousands of bottles with fancy labels. I then called the 3rd Army press camp with the following message, "Hey guys, how would you like a truck load of champaign for a big party?" The reply was a swift, "When can we get the bottles?" I gave them all the details and told them to send an Army truck down and that I would get it loaded for them. They decided to have a big party, since they had the necessary ingredients. The truck arrived from Luxembourg City, the Press Camp Headquarters, and I had it loaded with several hundred bottles. When the truck drove away, I mused, these guys will appreciate this great gesture and it will be great to come back there to hear about the big party. However, I was sent on a mission and didn't get back to Luxembourg until a week later.

When I did return, I expected a very warm welcome. This, I received but not in the way I expected. Instead the first correspondent I met when I entered the building told me, "You better not come in or they will kill you." Surprised, I replied, "That's a hell of a way to thank me for all the champaign for your party. "What party, he shouted, the champaign was green. Everything was ruined, so no party." At the time I didn't know but the champaign had not aged five years. The time necessary to insure a quality liquid. In the end, they believed me that I acted in their best interest and had not pulled a dirty trick as they originally thought I had done.

Billy Conn

Billy Conn, the Pittsburgh flash, was light heavyweight champion of the world. Both in 1941 and in 1946, he fought Joe Louis for the heavyweight title. Both times, he was flattened by possibly the greatest heavyweight fighter ever to enter a ring.

During the occupation of southern Bavaria, in the summer of 1945, the Army flew a group of American sports champions to Germany to entertain the occupation forces.

Billy Conn was a member of that troupe. It was my duty to

The author with Former Light Heavyweight Champion of the world. On top of 12,000 foot Zugspitz Mountain.

escort these champions around to the various units and to entertain them on sightseeing trips, as well.

One day, Billy Conn accosted me. "What's on the schedule today?" Before I could respond, he added, "How about doing something different - something special?" I thought for awhile and replied, "OK, Billy, I'll plan something special for your group, but I'll surprise you tomorrow with the plan."

The next day, I took the sport champions on a cog railroad trip up the Zugspite Mountain to the hotel atop Bavaria's highest peak. The view on that bright sunny day was spectacular. The Eibee Lake below looked, from the 3,000 foot level, like a small pond. At 9,000 feet, the cog rail train entered a 3,900 yard tunnel, cut through solid granite to its station inside the Schneefarnerhaus, atop the mountain. From here, you could see the Italian, Australian and Swiss Alps. It was indeed a spectacular view and the sports people were really impressed. "What do you think about this plan?," I inquired of Billy Conn as we stood on the observation platform at the hotel. "Great, super!," he exclaimed. "But there is more," I offered. Then, I escorted them to an elevator that would take us to the third floor and to the roof of the hotel. When we arrived at the new 'surprise' for the group, I led them into a cable car that was to ascend another 2,000 feet to the very top of the Zugspitz. The cable car, was at times, as much as 1,500 feet above the mountain slopes. The cable towers were mounted on peaks. The cable car swayed in the wind and was a truly scary ride. When we arrived at the top, we left the car to walk to a narrow observation point where we could see, it seemed, across the top of the world. After telling the group about a nearby building that, was the main German transmission station for all German submarine communications during the war and describing the Swiss Alps and Lake Constance, I led the group back to the cable car. Much to my surprise, I found that Billy never left the cable car.

"You really missed a spectacular view," I told him. He said nothing. When we finally arrived at our headquarters in Garmisch, everyone in the group thanked me for the days outing. Everyone that is except Billy Conn.

As he walked away he muttered, "You and your damn surprise!" I did not know that a man who fought Joe Louis, was evidently afraid of heights.

Next time, I thought, I had better outline the exact plans of the day for the group. After all, I didn't think it was advisable to have Billy Conn as an adversary.

German Field Marshal Wilhelm List

During March of 1945, the 10th Armored Division was attacking south into southern Bavaria. At that time the Allies were searching for German high ranking officers under whose command several atrocities were committed.

An officer friend of mine who was in the U.S. Third Army Counter Intelligence Corps came to me with a request that I join him in the search for German Field Marshal Wilhelm List. The Field Marshal had been in command of German forces that overran France, Poland and Czechoslovakia, was commander of all German forces at Stalingrad, and was responsible for atrocities at Malmedy, Belgium and at other places.

I told my friend that I would go with him to search for List. He had numerous leads that all proved fruitless. We questioned dozens of Germans in the area and finally obtained a good lead. After two days of toiling through the mountainous area, we located the field marshall. As I remember, his picture had been on the cover of *Newsweek* magazine earlier.

When we broke into the house where he had been hiding, his wife denied he was there. After a brief search we found him hiding in one of the upstairs rooms and brought him downstairs.

At that time, his wife screamed at us in German. I turned to him and asked, "What is she screaming about?" He replied that she thought we were going to kill him. She dropped to the floor and grabbed me around my legs.

"Tell her," I said, "that we were not going to kill him." She stopped crying and stood up. "We are going to take him to the prisoner of war cage in Garmisch," I continued. The field marshall had shed his uniform and was dressed in typical Bavarian garb of liederhosen. Haughty and ramrod straight, he demanded to know of me, "What right do you have to take me prisoner." Pointing my .45 caliber pistol to his head, I replied, "This is my right, any questions?"

We took him to the PW cage and to our astonishment, even though he was out of uniform, the German prisoners, about a thousand, all stood to attention. We were really not surprised knowing the discipline of the German soldier.

Before we left the house where List was captured, I took his family heirloom dueling sword, his medals, Lugar pistol and a portrait of him.

When I got back to headquarters, I reported to Major General William H.H. Morris that we had captured the field marshall. "Are you sure he is the field marshall wanted by the Army" he asked. "Yes sir," I replied. General Morris then called Corps Commander Walton Walker who had led the U.S. Third Army from the invasion to the Rhine River. Walker asked the same question, "Are you sure that it really is Field Marshal List?" Morris replied in the affirmative.

General Walker then called U.S. Third Army Commanding General, Lieutenant General George S. Patton who asked the same question. All went well until I had a call from a Patton staff officer I knew. "You may be in deep trouble," he offered. Surprised I asked why. He said when Patton interrogated the field marshall, he complained that the captain (me) had taken his heirloom dueling sword and portrait among other things.

Scared, I took the sword, medals and portrait and decided to return them to the house where they were taken. It was dark by then, and after a fruitless search I thought I would just throw them out of the jeep. Better sense prevailed, and I changed my mind. I kept them.

I never did hear anything more about the incident, much to my great relief. Though I realized later that I told the great lie when talking to the field marshall's wife. "Don't worry, I told her, your husband will probably be freed in several months." Since the war was expected to end by May, I really believed what I told her. But, I did not know at the time that the field marshall was one of the most sought after German officers because of atrocities committed. List was put on trial at Nuremburg and sentenced to life in prison. He died 17 years after the war in prison. To this day, I'm glad I never had to face Mrs. List again.

The Absent War Correspondent

While serving as a press officer in General George S. Patton's U.S. Third Army in Europe, a most unusual situation occurred. A war correspondent for a London tabloid was among the group of about one hundred correspondents.

His daily war communiqués back to his newspaper were exciting and often, very dramatic. My job was to brief some of the correspondents each morning on the battle plans for the day. Following that, he often escorted them to the front lines in press jeeps. After months on the job, he became suspicious of the British journalist when he read his brilliant descriptions of Allied battles. His suspicion was based on the fact that this particular war correspondent had never once been with the escorted writers to the battle lines.

It eventually developed that the British correspondent had not gone to the front the whole time he was in the press camp. Since there was so much activity at the camp and so many correspondents going out in different areas each day, nobody paid any particular attention to him.

This is how he worked out his "absentee" coverage of the front lines. He listened carefully to the daily morning briefings and then as the rest of the correspondents took off for the combat areas, he would hide somewhere with a bottle of scotch for company. When the correspondents returned, he would appear just as excited as the others about the days events. He would act as though he returned from the battle lines and would question the other writers. Following that, he would select what he considered the best war tales, sit at his typewriter and bang out his dramatic lines.

Needless to say, he was finally unfrocked and was kicked out of the press camp and later fired by his British tabloid. If he could have carried out his ruse a few more months, he would probably been given an award by his paper for his "on the battle scene" reporting.

Opportunity Knocks
(But Fate Did Not Answer)

I headed straight to New York City in November 1945 to seek a job. To possibly help me succeed, I wore my uniform as I made the rounds for employment.

One day, I was at Grand Central Station on my way to my brother's home, when a distinguished gentleman came up to me seeing my Division Patch. "I see you were in the 10th Armored Division." He continued, "did you happen to know my son, Major Stanley Resor?" I replied "Yes, I knew him well. He was an artillery battalion Commander."

"What are you doing here," he inquired. "Looking for a job," I responded. He then gave me his card and wished me luck. I thanked him and left. When I got home, my brother asked how things were going. I told him that it was another bad day. Later I casually mentioned the chance meeting with the distinguished gentleman earlier that day. "What was his name," my brother asked"? I searched my pockets and gave him the gentleman's card.

"You dummy," my brother exclaimed. "Do you know who he is?" "No," I replied. My brother who was in the advertising game told me that the gentleman was Chief Executive Officer of the J. Walter Thompson Agency; the largest ad agency in the U.S. Since I had been looking for a job in PR, media or advertising, this was the one big break for me that I nearly blew. The only reason the gentleman in question came up to me was because his son was a 10th Armored fellow officer.

The next day I called Mr. Resor and thanked him for his courtesy and asked if I might come to his office. He set a date and time. When I arrived there, I must have passed through three secretaries on the way to his spacious office.

He was very gracious and questioned me as to what type of job I wanted. After expressing my needs, he said, "We may have an opportunity for you as editor of the agency's internal newspaper and he arranged for me to meet with the personnel director.

After checking my qualifications, the director announced, "The job is yours, but there is one condition, if the former editor returns prior to December 1st, we will save his job for him." I understood and thanked him and hoped the former editor would choose another job at another agency. I went home with great excitement and great anticipation. The agency was to call me if the situation changed. Three weeks went by and it seemed to me that my chances were really good. Then, as I remember, on the last day of November before the deadline passed, I got the call that I didn't want. The former editor reclaimed his job the day before the deadline expired.

Incidentally, the young artillery major, Stan Resor, became Secretary of the Army in later years and invited me down to his office at the Pentagon.

I was very disappointed but I continued to search. A friend sent me to the City College of New York where I was retained as assistant to the president for public relations. This was an interesting stint for four years and it was very educational, especially because I lunched with the heads of all the departments and listened to their conversation about engineering, art, business, English, writing, math and other university areas. Later, new opportunities arose to enable me to form my own PR agency in New York and then in Louisville, where we moved in 1955. I continued in PR and fund raising until 1993 when I retired. My secretary, Elah Duemler, served with me as office manager for three decades. She was very efficient, loyal and helped contribute to our successes.

Lady Luck smiled at me then but luck deserted me as related to the ad agency, but then luck relented and gave me the opportunity for an excellent job. I would rather be lucky than good anytime. But it would be better to be lucky and good.

John Steinbeck - Margaret Truman

In New York City, where I served as a reserve officer for several years after I was discharged from the Army, I attended Reserve meetings. In my unit were editors of national magazines, radio and newspapers and newsreel executives.

One night after the meeting, a friend who headed a newsreel company asked me if I wanted to go to Sardis a Broadway restaurant that catered to the Broadway theaters people.

"I've got a date," he said "with Margaret Truman." I thought, oh sure, and I am Clark Gable. We went to Sardi's where we sat for some time. No Margaret Truman showed and I was about to leave when she joined us. She was a lovely person and very interesting to converse with. After a while, a man came over and sat with us. During all the excitement, I was introduced to him but failed to hear his name. We had a great conversation and I thought he was very interesting.

After some time, I left the party. The next time I saw my friend, Jack, I asked him who was that gentleman who joined us. "You dummy," he said "that was John Steinbeck, the author of *Grapes of Wrath* and other books."

John D. Rockefeller Jr.

While serving as the assistant to the president of the City College of New York in 1952, I was asked to manage the press relations for a big fund raising event at the Waldorf Astoria Hotel.

The principal speaker was John D. Rockefeller Jr. and several distinguished guests were also on the program. On the day of the event, I called Mr. Rockefeller's office to coordinate the reception and dinner.

When we all arrived at the hotel for the reception, I did not see Mr. Rockefeller. I called his office again and his secretary stated, "Don't worry, he is dressing on the train (this was a black tie event) and he will be at the hotel on time.

My job was to arrange photographs of the distinguished guests. I realized that time was fleeting before dinner and no Mr. Rockefeller present. I decided to finish the picture taking and advised the college president that we would be ready to enter the ballroom in a few minutes. I asked the photographer for one last picture and approached the president who was talking to a man I did not know.

I brought one of the distinguished guests with me for a last picture with the college president and said to the person he was talking with, "I'm sorry but I need to get this picture before we enter the ballroom." The gentleman replied, "No problem, go ahead." He moved aside.

Then we entered the ballroom. I was disappointed that Mr. Rockefeller had not shown up. When the dinner was over, the president introduced the head table and then the featured speaker who approached the podium.

I nearly died when the speaker was John D. Rockefeller, the man I pushed out of the picture. He was the one person I wanted to be photographed with the President.

After the event was concluded, I approached Mr. Rockefeller and apologized for my terrible mistake. "I'm so sorry I said, to have not recognized you in the reception room." He replied, "Oh, that is no problem," and he was very gracious about my goof. At the press table, one of the reporters found out about this goof and gave me a hard time - much deserved.

A Promising Career Lost

In the early 50s, when I served as special events director for the greater New York City Fund, I had been fortunate to a chance meeting with General Willis Crittenberger, my former military commander during World War II. The general offered me the job as special events director. He was a tall genial and a very intelligent person.

One day when I was in his office, he received a telephone call from President Eisenhower. He asked me to excuse him while he talked to the President. I left immediately. Later, he called me back to his office.

"I have great news," he announced, "Eisenhower has asked me to be the ambassador to Brazil." Then, to my great surprise, he casually said, "How would you like to go to Brazil with me as press officer at the U.S. Embassy there?" It took me about four seconds to answer, "Sir, I would like that very much."

President Roosevelt visits Tenth Armored at Fort Benning. Gov. Ellis Arnall of Georgia and Maj. Gen. Paul Newgarden, Tiger Division Commander. 1942.

During the next few weeks I began studying language tapes for Brazil. It was an exciting time for me, but I failed to note in the newspapers at the time that Ike was being criticized for appointing too many generals to ambassadorial posts.

About a week later, Crittenberger summoned me to his office once again. "Well," he said, "I have bad news." The President called this morning to say he had to withdraw the ambassadorial appointment because of extreme pressures by party big shots to demand that he appoint big time supporters to the much sought after ambassadorial post. Though with great reluctance, Ike had to go with the flow, so to speak. Not only did the General lose that great opportunity, but his press secretary to be, also fell to the political onslaught, unfortunately! All the language tape practicing for Brazil was never used!

President Harry Truman

The City College of New York had arranged for a special medal to be presented to President Truman at the college as part of the institution's centennial celebration in 1954 Unfortunately, though the President accepted the invitation, shortly after he had to cancel because of a conflict. As a result, the event was changed and we were to go to the White House a few weeks later for the medal presentation.

I remember well, at the time, the verbal abuse directed at the President by many who did not share his views, and I was one of those uninformed as to the President's abilities. When we arrived at the White House, President Truman was so very gracious. He took us to the Oval Room where he pointed out the many historical objects there and spoke eloquently about President Roosevelt who preceded him. "I'm interested mostly in peace," he said several times.

Harry S. Truman.

Unlike many presidents, he was very down to earth, pleasant and seemingly unaware of the awesome stature of President of the United States. He had narrowly defeated Tom Dewey earlier for the presidency.

My view of Mr. Truman was drastically changed as a result of hearing him and his hope for peace and for the welfare of the Country.

This is an example of how people view a presidential candidate based primarily on party affiliation and news reports. What people thought of him and what he was really like are two different views that are usually misinformed. Historians, 25 years later, rate him as one of our best presidents. And, he had to make one of the most awesome decisions as President when he ordered the bomb to be dropped on Nagasaki and Hiroshima in 1945.

The interesting thing about his decision, in my view, was that the bombing of the two cities saved both Japanese and American lives had the war continued.

Most of all, I believe that the atom bomb prevented World War III because the bombing was so final and the use of the bomb prevented both adversarial combatants from occupying ground - the objective of war to begin with. Other nations realized this and steered clear of nuclear warfare. This probably prevented another war and resulted in peace for more than 50 years, except for smaller wars, but no world war.

Cowboy Star

One of my clients in New York years ago was Roy Rogers. The Roy Rogers Rodeo at Madison Square Garden was a major event at the time. I had no problems promoting this show with the media and enjoyed working with Roy.

During that time, I was also doing sports promotion and often provided leads for Red Smith, syndicated sports columnist for the New York Herald Tribune, one of the two leading New York papers at that time. When the Roy Rogers show opened, I sent tickets to Red, his wife and young son. Red's boy was a great admirer of cowboys and was thrilled to go to the rodeo. I arranged with the cowboy to come by Red's

Author with Roy Rogers.

section and I lifted up the boy to Roy's saddle. When Red covered the Kentucky Derby at Churchill Downs he commented to me how very pleased he was for his son to be able to sit on Roy Rogers lap. Needless to say, his office door was always open to me because of the pleasure afforded his son. Red was a first class human being, a great sports columnist and a pleasure to work with.

After one evening's performance of the rodeo, Roy Rogers changed from cowboy outfit to a business suit and suddenly announced that we were going to drive to Atlantic City that night. We left before midnight and drove most of the night. At that time, there were no interstate roads. We walked the famous boardwalk and fiddled around until late morning and drove back to New York for his nightly rodeo show. The interesting thing about this little escapade was that only one person recognized Roy in his business suit at Atlantic City. We were walking on the boardwalk at 3:00 a.m. in the morning, a man approached and excitedly remarked, "You are Roy Rogers!" Roy replied, "Are you kidding? "Do I look like a cowboy?"

The Payroll Incident

As a young tank company commander in the Third Armored Division, which was training in the Mojave Desert in preparation for assignment to combat in North Africa in World War II, I was summoned to Battalion Headquarters.

The battalion commander was a no nonsense hardened cavalry officer. "Sit down, lieutenant," he commanded. "I have a job for you."

Then, very casually, he ordered me to pick up the division payroll at Indio, California for the 16,000 men of the division. It was as though I was to go to the corner drug store for a tube of tooth paste, the way he put it.

Nevertheless, I took this order very seriously and put together a pickup team of two tanks, two half tracks and a jeep and started out for Indio, California, located about 100 miles west of our desert camp.

When we arrived at the railroad station at nightfall, I put two armed guards on the roof of the station platform and dispersed six other guards around the station. After an hour, the train rolled into the station. I must admit, I felt somewhat important being entrusted with a multi-million dollar payroll.

As the train rolled and finally stopped, I walked to the baggage car where the baggage master casually asked me, "Are you here to pick up the division payroll, sonny?" I assured him that was my intention.

"Okay," he replied and soon the baggage handler was throwing out bags and bags of currency. I signed my name on a piece of paper for the baggage master. Then, my squad scooped them up and threw them in the two halftracks. I recalled the two guards from the roof and took off for our division headquarters.

When we arrived at our headquarters four hours later, I was surprised and very concerned that there was no headquarters there. The division had apparently suddenly departed for further maneuvers. As a result, we wandered around the desert for three days searching for the Third Armored Division. Most of the time, all we saw were desert jack rabbits that provided firing practice, but no hits. On occasion, we would come across another unit. "Have you seen the Third Armored anywhere," I inquired. The answer was "no."

Finally, on the fourth day, we found the division located some 200 miles from the original camp. When I approached my battalion commander, expecting praise for finding the "lost" division, his first words were "Where the hell have you been, lieutenant?" I explained the circumstances to him, but to no avail. I was assigned the worst possible job in the Army for two weeks. I was ordered to inspect the division latrines.

Ted Collins - Kate Smith
New York Yanks

Ted Collins was a top executive at Columbia Records and made a fortune there. In addition he discovered Kate Smith and was her personal agent for years. And, besides that, he bought the NFL Boston Bull Dogs Team and moved them to New York to compete against the New York Giants who, at that time, were an average team, coached by Mel Owens.

I was assigned to promote the New York Yanks which was a difficult job considering that the Giants were the team at that time. Ted Collins was a tough businessman and wanted immediate results. I flew to NFL cities in advance to promote the game and came back with the team after their road games. It was easy to arrange for interviews for the players in Washington, Philadelphia, Chicago and other cities, because the local media needed player personalities from both teams to stir up reader interest for the Sunday games.

Star quarterback for the Yanks was former Texas All-American Bobby Lane, but the Yanks did not have enough quality players to favorably compete against other teams and they won few games. The attendance was so weak that the ticket manager instructed his staff to "paper the house." This meant that ticket sellers sold alternate seats to create an impression that the stadium was full of people. Seating 25,000 seats then, helped make it look like there were more people there than there actually was.

One day while in the stadium office, he had a call from someone inquiring about game time. He was so disturbed about tickets sales that he said, "Sir, what time would you like us to start the game." I recall that year that the only game the Yanks won was against the Giants. I remember too, that then, the home team had to pay the visiting team $25,000 regardless of the attendance. Our team never had enough people in the seats for Ted to make a profit. That's why he sold the team to Dallas a year later and reportedly dropped more than a million dollars from that enterprise.

Ted named his son-in-law, Frank, as the team manager. Frank had been in the Air Force and he and I became close friends. We found a group of interesting people from West Chester County, New Jersey and Long Island and arranged group parties at all these places. Frank's wife was a great party giver and was a ton of fun. Sometimes she made not to flattering remarks about Ted, her father. I had had some trying times with Ted and offhandedly remarked one time, "He can sometimes be a real bastard." To my surprise, even though she made the same remark, she shot back at me, "How dare you call my father a bastard." I replied that she had made the same remark. Then she exclaimed, "I can say that but you can't." Ted had a room in his mansion with the walls covered with pictures of his celebrity friends. I think that was when I got the idea and as a result, my office den is wall to wall with pictures of the personalities I worked with during the five decades.

When Ted managed Kate Smith, who was a headliner at the time, she was responsible for his greatly enlarged bank account and, accordingly, she made heavy demands on his time. On several occasions she would call him at all hours of the night from her summer home at Lake George and demand that he come up there and now. This he did, not wanting to lose his lucrative account. Many people told me that Kate Smith was a very difficult person to deal with, a far cry from her All-American, apple pie image.

Our parties, as mentioned earlier, were very interesting because the people included all kinds of personalities from top executive to a truck driver who often came out with the darndest statements and was the life of the party. We each took turns in entertaining this group. I moved to Louisville in 1955 but still miss those great people.

Horace Stoneham
New York Baseball Giants

Six years after World War II, I joined Art Flynn Associates as account executive. One of our clients was the New York Giants Baseball Team, owned by Horace Stoneham.

Our agency was located at 59th Street Park. Horace Stoneham was a very heavy alcohol user. Often without notice, he would burst into our offices without warning, in a state of never never land. Sometimes he

Author as accountant Executive at Art Flynn Associates.

would go into the hotel telephone room and pinch the operators, a sport he seemed to enjoy. Then, not to offend the women operators, he would hand them $100 bills. Not surprising, they were pleased to see him come, the more often the better. Then, he would come to our office and disrupt our work. This happened often.

Finally, we found a way to get him to detour our office. By chance, we heard that he hated incense. Then, we made a deal with a couple of people in his office. "Call us," we asked, "Let us know when he is on his way to our office." When we got the call, we lit incense all over the place. When he arrived, he would smell the incense and very offended by the smell would leave abruptly. He never knew of the incense scam.

One time, he and two of us went down to a nightclub in Greenwich Village. We had a few drinks when he announced, "Let's get the hell out of here." He told me to get a cab, which I did. We drove three blocks to another nightclub. "How much is the fare," Stoneham inquired. "35 cents," the cabbie answered. Stoneham then directed me to give the cabbie $35, which I did. You can be sure that amount appeared on my next expense account.

Horace Stoneham was a very interesting, considerate and gentle man when he was sober, and he had a great baseball mind.

Willie Mays - Baseball

During my years in New York with an agency retained by the New York baseball Giants, the colorful and sometimes controversial manager was Leo Durocher.

When Willie Mays came up to the big leagues, he was virtually unknown. To my knowledge, he learned to hit by playing stickball in the New York streets. A player with a stick had to hit a small ball, which was a difficult feat. Apparently, this experience served Mays very well.

I also remember hearing from the players that one day in the clubhouse,

Willie Mays, New York Giants Polo Grounds (1951).

Durocher told Mays, "I don't give a damn if you don't get a hit the rest of the year." He continued, "you are my center fielder, period!" This conversation was a result of the fact, as I recall, that Mays didn't get a hit during his first 30 at bat. A few days later he connected for a home run and then went on a tear hitting over 300 with more than 30 home runs that year. As everyone knows, he went out to be baseball's premium center fielder.

Arguably, he was the best center fielder in baseball history. Rarely does a player emerge in baseball with enormous ability as Willie Mays. From 1951-1972, he hit 667 home runs.

Jackie Robinson

When I toiled for the New York Baseball Giants in the early 50s in New York, I was assigned to do an interview with Jackie Robinson, the first black player to play in the major league. We were at the Polo Grounds in New York that day when the Giants hosted their arch rival, the Brooklyn Dodgers.

Everything went well during the Robinson interview on the field before the game, until one of the Giant players, Monte Irvin, broke into our interview and joked with Robinson. At the time, it was no big deal, but when I got back to the Giants office, I was sternly reprimanded for the incident. At that time, opposing players were not allowed to fraternize on the field, (as compared to today when the athletes from both teams talk to each other when they are on the bases.) Sometimes the conversation was, "Where is a good place to eat" or "see you at

The author interviews Jackie Robinson prior to the Dodgers-Giants game at the Polo Grounds.

Toot's Shore's," a midtown sports bar and restaurant or other more personal discussions.

Jackie Robinson was not only a superb player but he was an intelligent, articulate and an interesting and superb athlete.

In the major leagues, players are often traded to other teams, so they get to know opposing players quite well.

One day, when the Giants played the Dodgers in Brooklyn, all you had to do was bring a musical instrument to be admitted (any kind of instrument.)

You can't believe the result of this event, and it was not to be repeated again. The sound of 25,000 musical instruments was deafening to the ears! Baseball players are a different breed than other athletes.

Their eye-bat coordination is superb. Especially when a 95 mile an hour fastball blurs across the plate. Baseball players are usually very good golfers because of their coordination.

Jackie Robinson was a one of a kind athlete and more, he opened the door to blacks, previously denied the opportunity to play in the big leagues.

A Day At The Races

While acting as an account executive for the Art Flynn Associates in the 50s in New York City, I was assigned to promote midget car racing at the polo grounds where a special track was installed inside the stadium. The races were not producing the anticipated attendance. One of the most important reasons for this problem was that the race car that got out in front always won because at high speeds, there was not enough rubber on the track...it was too dangerous for the outside cars to pass due to the lack of traction.

In any event, through a third party, I was able to secure Eddie Arcaro, the leading jockey at the time. My idea was to meet Eddie at the parking lot at Belmont Park when he was racing and get a news picture of him sitting in the midget race car in his track racing clothes.

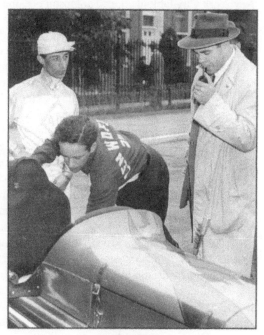

Eddie Arcado.

Earlier, I had poor luck in getting press coverage for the polo grounds midget track. As a result, I called the *New York Mirror*, a tabloid popular at the time, and talked to the sports editor. I said to him, "Would you send a photographer out to Belmont Park to take a picture of Eddie Arcaro in a midget race car?"

He laughed at the idea but replied, "If you can get Eddie Arcaro in a midget race car, which I doubt very much you can do, I'll put the picture on the front page."

I told him I did have a definite commitment and that I could produce Eddie for the event. His answer was "Okay," "I will send a photographer but I doubt Arcaro will show." Eddie did show, and the picture appeared on the front page as promised.

But, there was an unanticipated problem. The media director for the track showed up and yelled at me, "Get this race car out of here. What the hell do you think you are doing?" I told him I was sorry, but fortunately we had already taken the pictures for the *Daily Mirror*. I was under the impression, at the time, that I was totally unwelcome at Belmont Park forever. This is an example of some of the things an account executive has to go through to satisfy his client.

Lex Thompson

Though not known nationally except in adverse night club incidents in New York City tabloids, Lex Thompson became involved in sports enterprise. He was the owner of the championship Philadelphia Eagles NFL team in the early fifties.

His father left him eleven million dollars in drug stocks when he died. Lex came to New York City as a hard drinking (gin) playboy and invested in a risky project. He had an aluminum and board midget race track that was fitted into the Polo Grounds and could be removed when the N.Y. Giants played football. The cost of installation and removal was enormous.

What he didn't consider was that the elevated track favored the car that jumped out in front; this car always won because it was too dangerous for the outside cars to pass for lack of traction. This venture was a bust from the start, costing him several million dollars. Lex was a spoiled child. Tall and cocky, he alienated sports writers by offering misleading information. One was Red Smith, syndicated sports columnist for the New York Herald-Tribune. Not knowing this, I asked Red to interview Lex regarding his midget race track. Red agreed.

When we met at Toots Shore's restaurant, Red reminded Lex that he had lied to him on another matter. Taken back, Lex apologized and Red, the decent person that he was, did a column on Lex, more for me than for Thompson.

Lex had hired me as press manager for his sports projects and to promote him as a person as well. Our office was in Madison Square Garden. I had a staff of three. Lex would come in after 11:00 AM each day. The first thing he would do was pour a full glass of gin- his breakfast. He would complain about his night club antics as reported by the tabloids. There were weekly pictures on the front covers. He would rage at me for not keeping his pictures out of the tabloids. I took this abuse for a long time but finally it was too much and I told him, "You wouldn't be in this jam if you behaved yourself at night." Further, I told him, "Take this job and shove it!" We packed up our equipment and left our office thirty minutes later.

Lex did have at least one good quality. He sponsored the U.S. bobsled teams in two Olympics. He was a tragic poor rich boy who was not able to cope with his fortune. Several years later, he died in a rooming house in Brooklyn, penniless.

Actress Marjori Reynolds

In the early days of my military service, I was assigned by the Pentagon to act as a technical advisor on tank training films at Warner Brothers studio in Hollywood.

During my year there, I became friends with Jack Reynolds, husband of actress Marjori Reynolds. We played tennis on several occasions and enjoyed some very fine dinners together. Once I asked him, "Jack, how does it feel to be the husband of a major actress?" He replied, "You won't believe it but I see very little of my wife because she is up at six AM for make-up and on the set almost all day, every day."

He added, "She is so tired that she goes to bed very early." It is possible that most people are unaware of actors' demanding schedules that include early rising, intensive review of the day's script, shooting the film, and the stress of wanting their best performance. I met Marjori on several occasions and found her to be an intelligent, hard-working individual, but always her mind was on the next day's film shooting.

Ed Sullivan - Broadway TV Host

While in New York in the early 50s, I served as technical advisor for the Broadway war play at the Belasco Theater.

Herb Swope, former director of the *Playhouse 90* TV series, asked me one day if I could do some promotion for the play, knowing of my PR background.

I replied that I would try. Previously I had contacted Ed Sullivan who weekly had one of the most popular programs in the nation, (his show was first to book the Beatles). I had previously called him to ask him to include my clients on his show. He accepted them and was a joy to work with. He had given me his private phone number earlier. When I called him, he said, "Well, what have you got for me this time." I told him about Fragile Fox and that the play needed more exposure. After some discussion, he announced "O.K. I'll take Act III, which I have seen and liked."

When I told Herb Swope, he was delighted and talked about fitting the act to

Sullivan's show format. We all arrived on the night of the show featuring the cast of Fragile Fox.

I went back stage with the cast and saw first hand why Ed Sullivan was so successful. While back stage, I talked to a pretty young freckle-faced girl who was to follow our part in the program. She seemed quite nervous and understandably so, since this was her first big time performance. Her name was Debbie Reynolds.

Footnote: Ed Sullivan paid big money for most of the acts in his show, but for our group he got the appearance free, as was the case of other similar acts. Yet, he got at least eight top name actors in our show, all of whom later had their own TV shows. But, it was worth the promotion that "Fragile Fox" play received from this exciting night for all of us.

Jimmy Durante

In the early 50s, Jimmy Durante was the hottest things going in the entertainment industry. On one occasion, when I was involved in promoting an annual pro football exhibition game for the benefit of the Herald Tribune Fresh Air Fund for underprivileged kids, I met on the street in New York City, a fellow promoter who worked for NBC.

"What are you up to these days?" he inquired. I told him about the upcoming exhibition game between the New York Giants and the Los Angeles Rams at the Old Polo Grounds.

It was the 75th anniversary of the *Herald Tribune* and the newspaper wanted this game to be special. My friend's face brightened, "Maybe we could work out a joint effort," he suggested. He added, "We are looking for promotional ideas for NBC's 50th anniversary, the same year!"

As a result, together, we put together a big half-time show where NBC trotted out their top stars, including Jimmy Durante, Milton Berle, Sid Caesar, Mel Torme, singer, and a host of other top entertainers.

I, then, arranged a dinner at Gene Leone's Restaurant on the night of the game. Four big black limousines pulled in front of Leone's at 5:00 p.m. There were excited comments from the big crowd gathered in front of the restaurant as the big name entertainers entered Gene's place. There were also some boos when those waiting were pushed aside to let the show people in. A lavish spread followed by some clowning around on the part of Sid Caesar, with an enormous block of cheese.

When asked for a check for the dinner, our gracious host, Gene Leone, brushed it aside and instead gave me a check for $500 for the Fresh Air Fund.

Following the dinner, we proceeded to the Polo Grounds for the game. I escorted one of the Met's top singers to the center of the field for the playing of the *Star Spangled Banner*. When the band began playing the National Anthem, she sang, "*Oh say can you see...*" then, she panicked and forgot the words; 55,000 spectators buzzed. Had I known she was that poorly prepared, I might have said, "If you have a problem with the words, pause and announce, everyone sing." But I was too late with too little.

Durante was one of a dozen top entertainers performing at half-time. The master of ceremonies was comedian Milton Berle. Durante was on stage at mid-field, performing his famous "breaking up the piano routine. He played long after his scheduled on stage time."

Finally the game officials rushed over to me and yelled, "get that damned stage off the field. I went to Milton Berle to ask him to get Jimmy to end his act. "Are you kidding me" he said, "I can't do that." He continued, "You tell him." I went to the front of the stage to signal Durante to stop. My effort was ignored. He continued until he had wrecked the piano. The game officials were really teed off and I was the only target.

Rudy Valee

When I was working in New York City in the late 40s, I encountered my former Armored Division Commander, Lieutenant General Willis Crittenberger. "What are you doing these days?" he inquired. I told him that I had formed a small PR agency. "Come to my office soon," he replied, "I may have something of interest for you."

General Crittenberger, who retired after having served as Commander of Chief of the Caribbean Defense Command, had accepted a job as president of The Greater New York Fund. When I visited him at his office, he offered me a job as special events coordinator for the Fund. I accepted with thanks. One of my duties was to enlist a top entertainer to appear (without charge) at the annual award banquet where more than four million dollars was distributed to the leaders of the Protestant, Catholic and Jewish religious. As promised, I secured the services of Rudy

Valee, who at the time was a show headliner. When I visited him at his hotel room, he surprised and pleased me by accepting the assignment.

I reported this fact to the general, who at first, was very pleased. Later, he called me to his office to say he was very concerned about having Rudy Valee at the banquet. He was told by someone that Valee had a reputation for dirty talk in his night club act.

I was instructed to return to Rudy to caution him about bad language at the banquet, since the affair was attended by the archbishop, the heads of the Protestant and Jewish religious leaders. When I approached Rudy, he was incensed. "Who the hell are you to tell me what I can say at the banquet?" he raged at me. Fearing he would cancel, I did my best to make him understand. Finally, he calmed down and said, "Alright, damnit, I'll do the show." Relieved, I returned to General Crittenberger with his message. The show went on and Rudy Valee received standing applause.

Vice President Ted Agnew

Though Ted Agnew was much maligned as vice president of the United States he was a charismatic person and was loyal to his 10th Armored Division Veterans.

Ted was an excellent county judge in Maryland and so well liked he won the governor's race there before becoming vice president. He joined the 10th Armored Division at Fort Gordon, Georgia in 1942 as a young lieutenant in one of our tank battalions. He and his wife lived in a modest apartment in Georgia, then went over-

Ted Agnew.

seas with the division which fought in some of Europe's greatest battles. He was quiet, modest and very capable.

When he became active in politics and served as vice president to Richard Nixon, we have heard that he became trapped in the Nixon Watergate scandal. Though investigators had not targeted Ted in their research for wrongful activities against Nixon, their search turned up bribery facts against Agnew and he was brought down along with Nixon.

Agnew's wrong doing evidently began as county judge. At that time, he could not afford to entertain as required, so he accepted bribes to augment his income, though that is no excuse for his activities. We heard that he continued to accept bribe money after he became governor and then vice president.

He was an all out favorite with the 10th Armored until the bad things happened. He went to the Division Association Detroit Chapter to visit with the 10th Armored buddies and he hosted a reception for the 10th's Reunion at Baltimore at the State House. Many thought he would succeed Nixon as president because of all things, he was a strong advocate of law and order.

When I hosted a reunion for the 10th Armored Division in Louisville a few years back, he called me to say he planned to come for at least one day but he cautioned me not to say he was coming because of the riots taking place in Baltimore and Washington and hoped he could attend. I went to Fort Knox and got a Maryland flag to display in his honor. Then, at the last minute, he called to say things were getting worse and that it was impossible to attend our reunion. He was loyal to us throughout his career.

Bobby Riggs, tennis

During my years in New York, I was assigned to several sports promotions including Forest Hills Tennis. The agency assigned me to Bobby Riggs, the eccentric tennis star, for a special promotion.

Bobby Riggs had invented a way for a person to play tennis by himself. He rigged up a long elastic cord to a tennis ball. To demonstrate, we went to one of the New York side streets where he put up a moveable tennis net.

Then he hit the ball over the net and the ball flew back to him. He could bang the ball over the net in all directions and the elastic cord returned the ball to him every time. A large crowd gathered and he showed his tennis prowess for about an hour. We just happened to have the tennis items boxed for sale and a couple of reporters and TV people provided the promo needed for his invention.

I never knew anyone like him. He had a grin that reminded me of a clown, but his grin was all business and he did well with his venture. This all happened after he had won most of the big pro tournaments. Later he made news again when he challenged Billie Jean King, the women's champion. He played with one hand. She beat him on national TV.

The Crusty Senator
(Senator Wayne Morse)

In those early years in New York, I was retained by the Speech Association of America to promote their annual banquet. Their speaker was the fiery Senator Wayne Morse of North Dakota.

When I made my rounds of the New York media to promote Senator Morse's speech, I was unable to generate much interest since he was going to reminisce about his early years as a speech professor.

The New York Times, Herald Tribune and TV networks indicated they would be interested if he would discuss the national headline issues of the day. I returned to the senator with this information. Though reluctant, he said, "Well alright, I'll see what I can come up with."

I then told the key members of the media that the senator would address the issues of the day. That night at the banquet, I sat with news reporters and TV representatives at the press table at the Waldorf Astoria Hotel.

Senator Morse, when introduced as the key speaker, began his speech by saying to the huge audience, "I had planned to recount my experiences with you as a speech professor, but your press manager said that I should talk about something important." With that, the audience shook with laughter and I, as the press manager, slid down in my seat - pleased that the audience did not know my name. In the end, Senator Morse hit the next day's headlines and air waves and I earned my fee.

Edward R. Murrow

In New York in the early 50s, I was asked by the City College of New York, where I served as assistant to the president, to arrange for Edward R. Murrow of CBS to speak to a group of journalism students.

Ed Murrow spent two hours with us citing the need for absolute honesty and balance in news reporting. He was totally relaxed outwardly but at the same time, glowed with intensity in speaking about his craft. Though there were a few other

Press Conference with Edward R. Murrow, NBC.

broadcast journalists who prided themselves on high ethical standards of reporting, Murrow perched at the top of the integrity peak.

He was extremely articulate. His words were factual, concise and persuasive. He was, in short, an impressive personality even though we never saw a smile on his face when a humorous situation rose up from his remarks. He and his credo reflected what was important. I think he had a difficult time understanding why such a large segment of the population wanted entertainment that seemed so trivial to him.

Perhaps Ed Murrow was one of a kind or, at least, there were few broadcast giants like him then or even now. While he was visiting with us, he was a walking or sitting promotion for the cigarette industry. We remembered a series he did on *See It Now* where he advised his huge audience that smoking was bad for one's health. We felt that the intense pressures he faced would not permit him to stop smoking.

All in all, Ed Murrow was one of those few individuals who could and did trigger an element of reconsideration of a person's views on so many matters affecting personal lives. He was a monument to broadcast journalism that still stands the ruthless test of time. Unfortunately, he died of an overdose of cigarettes even though he warned the students not to smoke.

Bernard Baruch

Of all the outstanding personalities the author has been privileged to meet through the years in performance of his duties, Bernard Baruch was easily one of the most interesting and impressive individuals.

An advisor to several presidents in his long and distinguished career, Mr. Baruch, known as the Central Park Bench Statesman, was a kindly and thoughtful person. It was said that he became a millionaire before he was 30 years old, having been a runner on the stock exchange. He was a great philanthropist, having given large sums to his alma mater, the City College of New York and to New York University. Preventive medicine was one of his pet reasons for giving.

When I served as assistant to the president of City College, I was assigned to escort Mr. Baruch to a New York City hotel where he was the principal speaker. On the dais were a large number of celebrities, including Supreme Court Justice Felix Frankfurter; Joe Dimaggio, the great Yankee outfielder; the mayor; and some 20 other dignitaries.

Few people will remember that during the mid-50s, Mr. Baruch was the persistently sole voice in the nation, calling for a halt in inflation, which he constantly voiced at every opportunity. He was years ahead of other leaders in this regard and would be very pleased to know that his urgent message finally became reality some 30 years later.

At the banquet, Mr. Baruch, in listening to the numerous speakers, would turn down his hearing aid, perhaps in apparent boredom. Though he could not hear what other speakers were saying, he would applaud when they applauded.

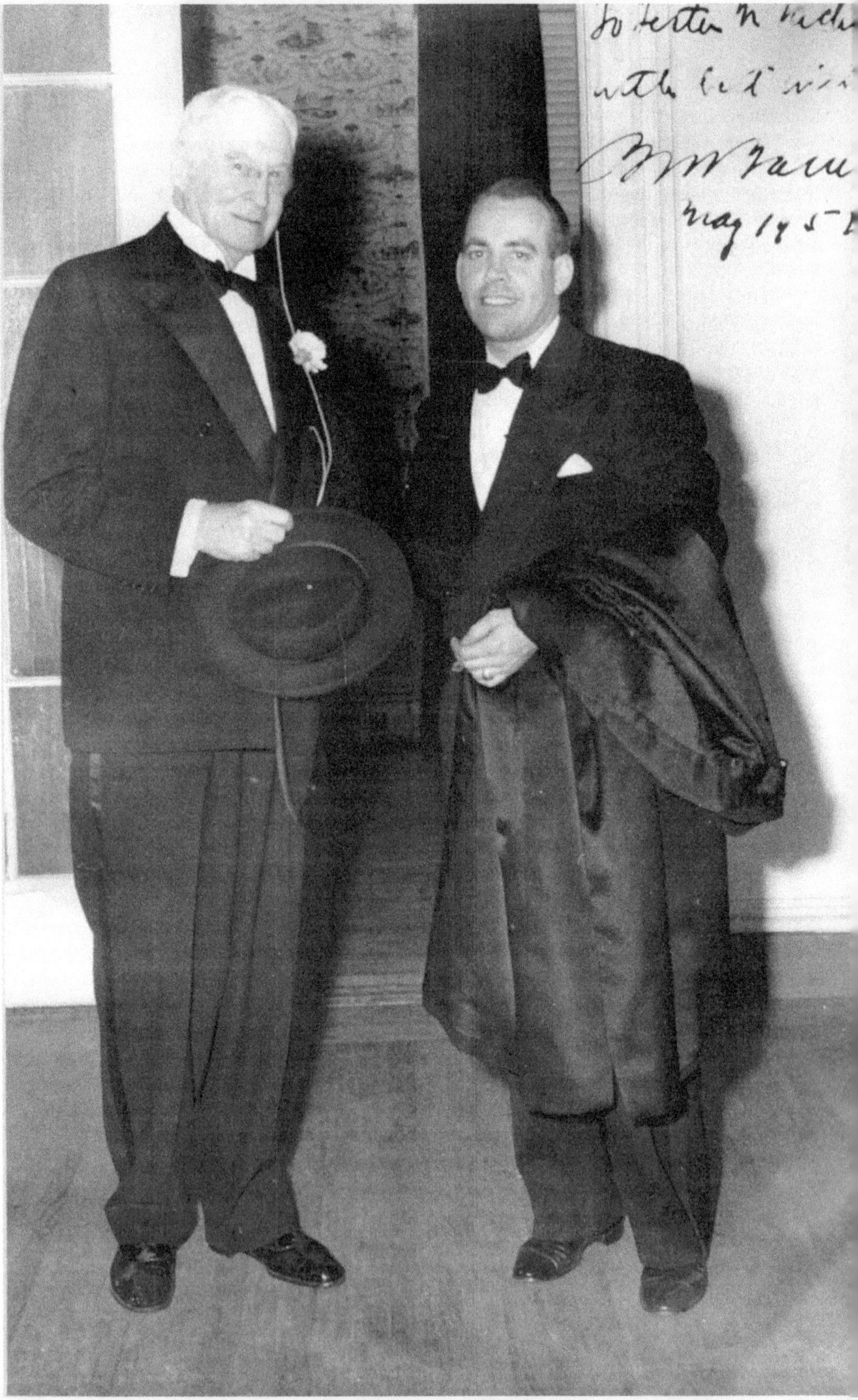

Prior to the banquet, he remarked to me, "I'm somewhat tired, will you arrange a room here for me at the hotel?" I made the arrangement as he requested and took him to his room. Though it was in September and still warm, he was wearing long johns when I helped him off with his clothes.

"Come back for me when it is time for me to speak," he requested. About an hour later I returned, helped him on with his clothes and escorted him to the ball-room. On the way, he told me that he wanted me to call his suite in the Waldorf-Astoria Towers and leave a message for the U.S. Secretary of Commerce that he would return to meet the Secretary at the Waldorf after the banquet.

I admired Mr. Baruch so much that I plotted to have a picture of us sometime during the banquet. I told Connie, our photographer, about this request, who assured me that this was no problem.

On the way out of the banquet with Mr. Baruch, Connie suddenly appeared in front of us and exclaimed, "Hold it, Sir, for a picture." Knowing that Mr. Baruch was in a hurry, I told the photographer, "No, Connie, Mr. Baruch does not have time!"

At that point, the elder statesman raided his hand and told Connie to go ahead and take the picture. "No problem," he remarked. Today, that picture is in my den, a proud remembrance of an encounter with one of the great intellectual personalities of this century.

Dane Clark

At the request of Lieutenant General William H.H. Morris, former command-ing general of the 10th Armored Division in Europe in World War II. I began re-search on a documented battle history of that crack "Tiger" tank outfit. Its 18,000 combat troops distinguished themselves by capturing 650 towns and cities in a ram-page across five European countries and netted 56,000 German prisoners, as well. The 10th Armored was General George S. Patton's spearhead armored first as it rolled at breakneck pace from France all the way to the Czech and Australian borders.

After seven years of research, the author's book *Impact* was published in 1955. It received critical approval in the *New York Times* Sunday Book Review.

At the time of the *Times* review, a veteran TV director, Herb Swope (of the *Playhouse 90 Series*) was looking for a Broadway war play to direct. Mr. Swope located a promising young playwright, Norman A. Brooks, who wrote the kind of play Herbert Swope wanted to direct.

Though the play received many accolades, its problem was probably that it was produced too soon after the war. The play's cast included a dozen actors headed by Dane Clark, Jim Gregory and others who went on to fame in their own TV series, movies and other plays. The day after the *New York Sunday Times* book Review of *Impact*, Herb Swope invited me to lunch. The invitation came as a result of the book review. Swope wanted a technical advisor for *Fragile Fox*, his new war play. After some discussion, I was retained by the producer to help make the final version of *Fragile Fox* as realistic as possible.

Dane Clark - Don Taylor. Broadway war Play 1953. "Fragile Fox."

During rehearsals for the play, I would give notes to the director for citing various words or actions that detracted from the authentic military plot.

Usually, the director would pat me on the arm and say, "Les, I think it would be better for you to mention these suggestions to the actors." Since I was a military expert, but a theatrical novice, I had some reservations about how to approach the actors.

First to be confronted with my suggestions was Dane Clark. I casually mentioned, "Dane, don't you think you should appear on the stage unshaven?" "After all, you are an infantry company commander cut off for days by the German army." I continued, "and you should wear a helmet instead of your dress cap."

His anger slightly under control, Dane replied, "What the hell is the matter with you? Do you not understand theatrical license?"

I replied that I did, but in this case, as a war play - any of the veterans returning from the war who viewed *Fragile Fox* would burst out laughing at some unrealistic aspects of the actors' lines, clothes and some of their stage actions.

This did not satisfy Dane Clark and he continued his ways despite my protests to the director. Herb Swope handled the cast with kid gloves. In the end he was right.

My list of suggestions was building at each rehearsal but they, mostly, were ignored. One of the suggestions was that the helmets the actors wore should be covered with camouflage nets, as they were in battle. This suggestion, like many others, fell on deaf ears.

I was beginning to have doubts about my assignment, that is, until the play opened on Broadway. The reviews were mixed, some critics gave rave reviews, but the key comments by the *New York Times* critic hurt the plays chances of success. I had no idea, up to then, how critical to a play were the reviews of the *Times* and *Herald Tribune* to success or failure, despite the reviews of a dozen other key critics.

Much to my surprise and undeniable pleasure, the play's reviews centered on one of the lesser actors, entirely because of his credibility as an actor in wartime. His grizzled appearance and dress, the critics, stated, made the story more believable.

From the day the reviews appeared, my job became much easier. Some actors actually sought out my advice. Dane Clark and Don Taylor used my own tank combat outfits brought home from the war.

Dane Clark did not shave, the other actors appeared on stage more realistically as soldiers, rather than as actors.

To create a better "war" atmosphere, I went to a downtown fishing pier, bought yards of fishing net and had the wardrobe lady dye the nets green.

The actors, this time, accepted the netted helmets without complaint. In fact, the job was becoming very pleasant. Friendships began to blossom and I looked forward to watching the play at least three or four times weekly.

Then, it all went down the drain and what happened next was almost unbelievable.

Among other duties, I was also assigned as safety officer. There were many opportunities for accidents, since rifles and pistols using blanks were used extensively in the play.

I had learned to enjoy Dane Clark's company and at the same time, I respected his ability to electrify the audience. He was perfectly cast in the role he played. One night, I visited him in his dressing room, as I often did, to discuss the play or other subjects. He had just come out of the shower and was in his shorts. As he talked, I picked up his .45 caliber pistol and casually handled it. Then it happened - for some unaccountable reason I pulled the trigger. Fortunately the gun barrel was pointed down but still the blast barely missed Dane's lower body. He nearly went through the roof. The gunshot sounded like a cannon blast in the small dressing room.

Everyone in the cast rushed to Clark's room, thinking the worst, though it was a blank round. Then, Dane Clark took dead aim at me, turned to the others and exclaimed, "Now what do you think of our great Major Nichols, our safety director?" All I could do was stand there in total embarrassment. When they all realized no one was hurt, they burst out laughing - everyone that is, but Dane Clark.

"Please," he insisted, "Do me a favor and visit someone else's dressing room from now on."

From that night on, I was never allowed to forget "safety aspects" of the play.

European Battlefield Tours

In 1967 several members of the Executive Committee of the 10th Armored Division Association asked me to organize a battlefield tour to Western Europe.

I had no experience in taking on this type of project, but decided to investigate possibilities. I called several agencies and found that a 17 day tour cost was excessive (at that time and value of the dollar). The following year I visited my brother in New York and was invited to play a round of golf at the Westchester Country Club. One of the men in the foursome was Fred Fugazy of the travel agency in New York. I told him of my desire to organize a European tour. His reply, "no problem." Since my flight home was Monday, the next day, it presented a problem of time. "Don't worry about it," he answered, "I'll send a limo to pick you up and we can resolve this project in time for your flight departure."

We met in mid-morning, worked out all details and I was driven to the airport in time to board my flight. The interesting part of this account was that we completed all arrangements in less than two hours. It was a 21 day tour and the cost was $950 per person! Their were 35 people that went on that tour to Germany, Austria, France and Switzerland. As a novice, I tried to give everyone as much experience as possible. The result - I rushed the group virtually every day to another hotel. Another destination. No one complained but we returned to New York's Kennedy Airport with a very tired group of travelers.

Since then, I organized and directed 15 European tours with as many as 115 people on one of the tours. We averaged about 75 people on each tour. At first, mostly men joined the tours and then on future tours the men brought their grown-up children. After the first five tours the Veterans began bringing their spouses, and I enjoyed listening to them describe their experiences to their wives. They would explain, "This is where I was hit, or captured or wounded," as we drove through battlefields in France, Germany, Belgium and Luxembourg. I really enjoyed listening to their accounts knowing that these men had previously described their battlefield experiences to their wives, who really could not visualize what their husbands were describing as they had not been at the battlefield site.

During the past three decades I was privileged to escort more than 1,200 veterans and their families on 15 European tours.

I learned after the first three tours to schedule less events, and to spend at least two to three days in the same hotel so they could gather more energy. During the last six tours I had to schedule less walking for my veteran friends since we were all in our "golden years" and many had difficulty walking. On the last four tours, I scheduled four to five nights in the same hotel in different cities to accommodate the wishes of our group members. We would go out each day and return to the same hotel.

Incidentally, the cost of the tours from $950 per person for 21 days in 1967 rose to $3,000 or more for a 17 day tour in 1996. This is a progression of the value of the dollar.

Highlights on the tours included the countries of Spain, Holland, England, Germany, France, Belgium, Switzerland, Austria and Luxembourg. Our actual battle areas were in France, Germany, Luxembourg, Belgium and Austria. The other non combat countries were added particularly for the wives who, of course, would rather visit Vienna, London, Paris, Madrid or Amsterdam. This is not to say that the men did not enjoy the same cities!

Other highlights included big ceremonies in France, Belgium and Luxembourg where the entire population turned out to honor the veterans. One of the most memorable experiences was to have men and women, who could not speak English, express their feelings with the only words they knew which was "thank you."

We had receptions everywhere in the cities in our combat areas in World War II and we laid about a total of 100 wreaths at various monuments honoring American soldiers. We had at least 60 receptions at city halls in Luxembourg, Metz, France and Bastogne, Belgium (the center of the bloody Battle of the Bulge in which 17,000 Americans were killed and thousands more wounded or captured).

The Battle of the Bulge was hailed by Prime Minister Winston Churchill, at that time, as America's finest hour. Actually, the Bulge was the scene of the greatest and most costly war in American military history.

Our last European tour, our 16th, was in September 1998 with 75 registered to go. Unfortunately for me, I was hospitalized and had not recovered sufficiently to go with the group. My friend, Henry Thompson of the Second Armored Division, agreed to act as spokesman for the group. I had numerous letters and calls from the group stating they had a wonderful time which I appreciated so much since I had spent part of a year and one half planning and arranging the itinerary, hotels, ceremonies, etc. As chairman of the Council of Armored Division Associations since 1996 (16 U.S. Armored Division Associations with a total membership of 32,000), I included six other Armored Division Association members beside the 10th Armored Division for the 1998 tour. I think my real value arrangements for the tours was what not to do as well as to do. We made long time friends in Belgium, France and Luxembourg as a result of the tours.

1969 Bastogne. Mayor Lawerence Oliveia.

And, it was interesting to note that tour members made great friends as a result of being together in close contact for periods of the weeks they traveled together. Finally, I am so glad I was asked to arrange these tours almost four decades ago!

Veterans Of The Battle Of The Bulge

In December 1994, the annual meeting of the Veterans of The Battle of the Bulge gathered together (1,900 Veterans) at Saint Louis for a major celebration of the 50th anniversary of the Bulge.

Speakers included Crown Prince Phillipe of Belgium; Crown Prince Henri of Luxembourg; Secretary of Defense, William Perry; chairman of the Joint Chiefs of Staff, John Shalikasvilli; Ambassadors from Luxembourg and Belgium and a host of three and four star generals. Though a big parade had been scheduled, it was canceled due to rain.

A ceremony at the St. Louis Cathedral was held that will never be forgotten. Other events also made this probably the biggest celebration of the Bulge anywhere in the nation. Organizers of this event did a masterful job!

I was given the opportunity to meet with the Crown Prince of Luxembourg who will soon become the Grand Duke. Tall and very distinguished, he was charming and very informed of the role of the 10th Armored Division which was credited with preventing a second occupation of Luxembourg. In 1944, I was taken to the palace by my commanding general of the 10th Armored to meet Grand Duchess Charlotte who thanked General Morris and the 10th Armored for saving Luxembourg from the German troops.

Front: Bob Wilson, Charlie Becker, John Sheffield, Priscilla Newgarden (widow) of Maj. Gen. Paul Newgarden), Les Nichols. Back: Ray Reed, John Dolan, Ralph Schmitz, George Ritchie.

General John Shalikasvilli, chairman of the Joint Chiefs of Staff at St. Louis, December 17, 1994 attending the 50th Anniversary of the Battle of the Bulge Ceremonies.

Bill Perry former Secretary of the Defense.

50th Anniversary of the Battle of the Bulge attended by 2,000 veterans of the bulge at St. Louis on December 15-18, 1994. Shown is Crown Prince Phillipe of Belgium.

White House presentation of Centennial Medal.

Then, in 1944, I escorted 115 veterans of the 10th Armored on the 14th European Tour. Ceremonies were held at Hanm, Luxembourg at the American Cemetery (where General George S. Patton is buried).

On that occasion, Grand Duke Jean laid a wreath at the cemetery. He asked me to pick out five 10th Armored veterans that he wished to meet. As they shook hands with him and during short discussions, when they told him what cities and states they were from, he seemed very knowledgeable and was very charming.

At the Battle of the Bulge ceremony, I told his son Henri about meeting both

Crown Prince Henri orf Luxembourg.

Grand Duke Jean, Luxembourg at American Cemetery at Hamm, Luxemberg. Author's book "Impact" presented to him as historian Jean Milmeister watches.

Dedication Ceremonies at Bastogne, Belgium McAullife Square on August 15th, 1994. Les Nichols, tour director and Tenth Armored Division Veterans Association Historian.

Arlington National Cemetary Ceremony. Tomb of the Unknowns. Washington, D.C. September 1, 1962. PArticipants; Tenth Armored Division Association: Lt. Col. Lester M. Nichols, President; Lt. Gen. W. HH. Morris, Jr. Division Commander.

his mother and father during a period of 50 years. I think it is possible that I may be the only veteran over that period to meet his entire family. And at Saint Louis I had the opportunity to meet Crown Prince Phillipe of Belgium, who too, was fluent in English and was also very charming.

Back to St. Louis in 1994 again. I was so impressed with Secretary of Defense William Perry, who was also a very interesting and down to earth intellectual. There too, I met and talked with the then chairman of the Joint Chiefs of Staff. When he spoke in the grand ballroom of the hotel, every seat was taken. The overflow crowd were watching the ceremonies on TV in an adjoining room. General John Shalikasvilli was the only speaker who took time to address the overflow crowd and was warmly greeted by everyone. I think it is unlikely that there will ever be a celebration of the Battle of the Bulge as huge as this event was.

Hostess Anita Madden

For 26 years, one of my agency accounts was the Kentucky Heart Association. I enjoyed this time even though I traveled 700 cities, towns and hamlets seeking volunteer chair persons for the annual campaign. I drove close to 30,000 miles annually. One of my favorite counties was Fayette; it was always a source of excellent leadership. The chairman in Fayette at that particular time was County Judge Executive Robert Stevens, who later was elected to the state supreme court and is the chief justice of the court at this time.

One day, he came to me with a suggestion, "Anita Madden," he said, "might be interested in including the Heart Fund as a recipient of proceeds from her annual super bash party." Her affair draws dozens of Hollywood, political, sports and business personalities each year. She is known as a national hostess with a flair for the unusual.

Bob and I met with her at a Lexington restaurant shortly after. After considerable discussion, she agreed to include sponsorship of the Heart Fund at her parties. I met her many times regarding Heart Fund arrangements. Though more than a few people regarded Anita as something of a "Hollywood" party giver, in fact, she is a very smart lady with a great business acumen. She is also a charming person and she provided the Heart Fund with much needed support. She and Preston have a beautiful horse farm in Lexington where they breed horses including some that have captured major stake races around the country.

Tribute to Les Nichols from Anita Madden. "working with Les Nichols on the Derby party for the past three years has brightened my days, lightened my heart and shown me that there are winners other than those at the races. He's terrific."

Her main effort these years have been in support of Boys Ranch. Anita is a credit to the thoroughbred industry. The first time we were invited to her annual Derby Eve party, the invitation announced "black tie." I did not pay much attention to the invitation and came to the party in a white formal jacket. Much to my embarrassment, I was about the only one there dressed as I was. Of course, no one said anything but I felt effect of not complying with the "black tie" invitation.

The next time, you can be sure that I was properly dressed for her occasion.

Louisville, Kentucky

Of all the places I have lived or served during the war years, we have enjoyed Louisville most of all. The reason? Kentucky is a state of personality with its rich heritage of pioneers, its topography, its people and its climate. I have lived in California (Army), Louisiana (Army), Illinois (Army), Washington, DC (Army), Georgia (Army), New York, Pennsylvania, Wisconsin, Colorado, New Jersey and North Dakota.

I was stationed in Fort Knox, Kentucky on three different occasions and became familiar with Louisville and liked it so much, I thought that some day, I might want to live there. As fate would determine, while I was working for an agency in New York, I was sent to Louisville to hire Paul Whitman, who, at the time had an agency here. However, Paul who was the treasurer and political advisor for the state Republican Party and had a contract with the Kentucky Heart Fund, Sts. Mary and

Author getting award from Kentucky Department of Tourism presented by Gov. Brerton Jones.

Elizabeth Hospital (building fund and other accounts) was not available. I thanked him for our visit and was leaving to go back to New York. Before I left, however, he offered me a job with his agency. "Thank you," I responded, "but no thanks." "Well," he said, "if you ever want to come with me, call me." I told him I would consider his offer. Nearly a year went by - a year of constant wearing travel. I practically lived out of a suitcase. It was then, that I decided to call Paul. "Sell your house and come as soon as you can, he said.

Thus, another door of opportunity appeared. I moved to Louisville in October 1955. It was by far the best move career wise that I ever made. And, I don't ever expect to move anywhere again.

Unfortunately, in 1958, Paul was planting a tree at his newly built home and died instantly of a heart attack. He was one of the smartest and most interesting men I had ever met and I have missed him greatly.

When he died I seriously thought of moving back to New York. However, when his clients suggested I stay and take over his accounts, I agreed. During the years since, I expanded the agency with several new accounts including the Kosair Children's Hospital, the Kentucky Hotel Association, the Louisville Hotel Association, the Louisville baseball Colonels, the Baptist College campaign, the Arthritis Foundation and other clients.

I retired from my agency in 1993 after having raised nearly 20 million dollars from the fund raising efforts. The Kentucky Heart Association was helped by every governor since 1965. Their support of the heart campaigns was instrumental. And, the Kentucky Women's Clubs led by Chloe Gifford, the president, were very prominent as well. Bob Stevens, then Fayette County judge, was also a major factor. Bob was elected state attorney general and later became chief justice of the Kentucky Supreme Court. Attorney Phil Ardery was a squadron commander and rose to the rank of major general, was also a key factor during some 30 years of the state-wide Kentucky Heart Campaign. But most of all the chairmen in 752 towns, cities and hamlets along with their volunteer workers were key to the campaign.

In addition, the Professional Women's Clubs of Kentucky also contributed to all the successful years. Governor Martha Lane Collins of all the governors devoted her expertise and efforts as well. Uppermost in my mind were the thousands of volunteers who generously supported the heart fund without any wish for publicity were good reasons why I enjoyed those years, traveling in Kentucky to every town, city and hamlet during the campaigns.

VSP Volunteers
(Very Special People)

During my travels in American and Western Europe over the past six decades, I was fortunate to be involved with famous people during my professional career. However, the people I respected most were literally thousands of volunteers that I worked with in fund-raising campaigns in New York and Kentucky. These women and men devoted long hours of service raising money for health, welfare, and educational purposes. These volunteers receive so little credit for their efforts, nor do they want credit.

Their efforts have literally provided hundreds of millions of dollars so that research could be expanded to save lives. For example, I truly believe there would have been no heart-lung equipment that has saved countless lives, very little support for the hungry and the homeless, and in general so many lives would have had a far different result were it not for these wonderful volunteers.

More specifically, I was so lucky in Kentucky to have the opportunity to become involved with the Women's Club of Kentucky, the Business and Professional Women's Club, and the Rotary, Lions, and Optimist Clubs. I have often speculated what life would be without these volunteers. The newspapers and TV stations show violence all the time. Gloom and doom.

BUT, what about volunteers? Yes, some volunteers are given honor on occasion but what about the "rank and file" volunteers? Traditionally too, a mere twenty percent of the population volunteers their time on behalf of the rest of our society.

America probably does more in volunteerism than other country, and even so, these volunteers represent a small percentage of the population.

Of all the famous people and interesting personalities I worked with during my sixty-year career, again, I feel personally indebted to these sent-from-heaven volunteers. Their rewards? Probably not on earth. Hopefully, in heaven.

Former Secretary of Defense
Cap Weinberger

When the former Secretary came to Louisville in 1987 as the featured speaker at the national convention of the military order of world wars, I was assigned as media chairman. We found the Secretary was very pleasant and most interesting. He brought his military aide with him (who was difficult to deal with- especially when the Secret Service scoured the entire hotel for security reasons). I set up a press conference and told the major that I would like to present my book "Impact," about the Tenth Armored Divison. "No, no way," he ordered. But, during the pre-dinner reception,

Cap Weinberger.

I gave my book to the Secretary. Not only did he thank me for the book, but he wrote a letter of thanks during his flight back to Washington. Sometimes, low-level aides take on a rigid stance for no reason in lieu of common sense. The Secretary in his letter stated, "I read most of 'Impact' on the return flights and enjoyed it very much."

The Lodging Industry

This section is offered for the interest of those travelers staying at hotels in Kentucky. This is a review offered to give hotel guests a better view of what the lodging industry is really like besides the guest seeing only the front desk clerk and the housekeeper. They are the tip of the lodging iceberg when they check in.

The most successful hotels in Kentucky and in the nation train their employees very carefully in guest satisfaction and great attention to detail. Small problems often can result in big issues. I joined the Kentucky Hotel-Motel Association in 1969 under contract as executive director, and also the Greater Louisville Motel-Hotel Association in 1975. During the past decade, I saw great changes in the lodging industry. In the 60s and 70s there were mostly large hotels. In Kentucky in 1960 there were 42 hotels which served as the meeting places where people gathered for local meetings, news, dinners and special events. There were only two motels plus the numerous tourist courts and mom and pop properties.

Then, in the late 70s great changes occurred, including the introduction of motor inns, motels, country inns that were built because of the introduction of inter-state highways.

One of the first companies to take advantage of the new convenient roads was the Holiday Inn chain developed by Kemmons Wilson whose vision of reasonably priced rooms, good location and restaurant services and affordable for traveling families resulted in a flood of chain properties. In Kentucky alone, from 1960 to present, more than 2,000 lodging properties were built. During the past two decades, the industry witnessed a new phase called segmentation. Big lodging chains began to offer three to four price levels which included the economy property, adding mid-priced, first class and luxury hotels with the idea of offering rates to appeal to the pocketbook of almost all travelers. When the nation went from the industrial age to the service industry millions of jobs were created.

Now, back to why hotels or motels were successful. The reasons, of course, were that these properties knew what it takes to keep guests coming back. What did they do? They made sure that the staff was competent and well trained to make sure that the guest's comfort and needs were met. The staff was given extensive training in quality assurance, safety, security, cleanliness and justified rates. Yet, there was one more important factor called employee retention. Long time employees were better able to meet the standards that the guests required than new employees.

At the risk of offending some of my great friends who manage excellent hotels and motels across Kentucky, (during my 30 years in this industry I was privileged to meet so many really fine managers. Actually, I worked with more than 300 across the state and provided more than 50 seminars on housekeeping, front desk procedures, security, fire safety, computers and other training seminars). Of all the hotels in Kentucky, I was most impressed with The Executive West Hotel in Louisville and its manager, Charles M. Beeler (who is, incidentally, my friend), but this is not why I felt that the Executive West Hotel probably has one of the very best employee retention programs in the state. Of course, there were many other properties as well, who are doing a great job in all aspects of management.

Why has the Executive West Hotel succeeded so well? It begins with the manager and the key is loyalty. To develop loyalty among employees, the manager must be loyal to the employees as well. Over the past 20 years, I have seen loyalty at its best at Executive West.

Building loyalty requires several things, among these are selection of employees, instilling a sense of security for them, decent wages, providing an atmosphere of satisfaction, and above all, praise for jobs well done. Employee retention is a problem for all properties yet, few of them match Executive West in employee retention. How do they cope with this problem? They, the employees at Executive West through the years have volunteered to put on special events, to include "roasts," shows, Halloween parties, attention to birthdays, anniversaries, and in effect, work as a team - all this because they respect and care for their manager who, in most cases, had not even asked them to do all the things they do as volunteers.

The end result? In working together on the job and off the job, they become better friends, and they develop a great sense of pride. This is why The Executive West Hotel, in my opinion, has probably the best employee retention in the state. And employee retention is a key to success! Since this was written, Charlie Beeler has retired and is living in Sarasota, Florida.

Speaking of Kentucky, you might be interested to know that although Kentucky is a relatively small state compared to other big states, has more counties than the bigger states. Why? Because in the early 1800s the State Legislature voted to have 120 counties. In this plan, no voter would have to ride a horse more than 30 miles to any county seat to vote.

And, a not so trivia statement, why limestone plays a major factor in Kentucky industries. Kentucky, the leading thoroughbred state in the world has its horse farms along streams that flow through limestone thereby a key to the race horse's delicate leg bones which are strengthened by limestone water. Then there is the bright leaf tobacco industry here that also gets its flavor from limestone waters. This is called bright leaf tobacco. Kentucky, at one time, was the largest coal producing state in the nation. Again, when you find great limestone deposits you will find coal. And, finally, to the delight of many Kentuckians, there is bourbon whiskey. Bourbon's flavor is influenced by the limestone filtered ground water which rests beneath so many world respected distilleries.

Kentucky Hotel Association presents distinguished Service Award to Les Nichols for 25 years service. Making award was Bill Walton, former Chairman of the board, Holiday Ins of America. Also in picture Bob Stephens former president of KY Hotel Association.

Elaine Estes President, American Hotel Association. 1991. Author recieves National Award Plaque.

Chief Justice Robert Stevens

In Frankfort at the annual meeting of the Kentucky Hotel and Motel Association, I was honored with a roast by the hoteliers for my 25 years as executive vice-president of the group. As usual, a Roast can be a very humiliating event for anyone, but all in good fun

Bob Stevens was Fayette County Judge at the time and was asked to be the master of ceremonies. He and I were good friends as a result of our working together on the Kentucky Heart Fund. He was Fayette County Chairman and I was state campaign chairman for the Kentucky Heart Association.

The night of the Roast at the Frankfort hotel went smoothly until several roasters ignored their time limits to greatly prolong the event.

"When is this thing going to end" he remarked. I don't have all night to spend here" and, "besides our daughter is to have a baby at anytime tonight."

Fortunately, the birth held off in time for Bob to be present at the blessed event. He was very kind to put up with the situation but told me, "next time you have a roast, please get someone else to M.C. the event!"

Former Chief Justice, Robert Stevens, KY, Supreme Court presents Distinguished Service award to the author.

Author's Family, Reisenstadt, Austria. September 1996.

Edie Nichols receiving citizenship.

Lt. Gen. William H.H. Morris looks on as Secretary of the Army, Stanley Resore presents award to the author.

Author with daughters Karen and Nancy.

Ed Hasenover, former famed Restauranteur, is honored by theTourism Industry. Left to Right: Paul Luersem, Les Nichols and Bob Stephens.